PURIFIED

CHRIST'S BRIDE MADE READY

BY
JONATHAN MACNAB

Purified

Copyright © 2021 by Jonathan Macnab

All rights reserved. No part of this book may be reproduced in any form or by any electronic or mechanical means, including information storage and retrieval systems, without permission in writing from the publisher, except by reviewers who may quote brief passages in a review.

Unless otherwise noted, all Scripture references are taken from the New King James Version®. Copyright © 1982 by Thomas Nelson. Used by permission. All rights reserved.

ISBN 978-1-7320417-2-1

Printed in the United States of America

First Printing, 2021

Story Reborn Publishing
P.O. Box 775
North Wilkesboro, NC 28659

www.storyreborn.com

This title is also available as an e-book at most online retailers.

"This life is a dressing room for eternity – that's <u>all</u> it is!" — Leonard Ravenhill

"Now this is eternal life: that they know you, the only true God, and Jesus Christ, whom you have sent." — John 17:3

"...who can endure the day of his coming, and who can stand when he appears? He is like a refiner's fire..." — Malachi 3:2

Table of Contents

Preface	
Prologue	1
Chapter 1 – Remembering Our Anniversary	6
Chapter 2 – Keeping Our Vows	16
Chapter 3 – The Groom	30
Chapter 4 – Knowledge of the Holy	43
Chapter 5 – Jesus Makes the Journey	58
Chapter 6 – For Better or Worse	67
Chapter 7 – Tried and True	84
Chapter 8 – A Covenant People	98
Chapter 9 – In or Out?	115
Chapter 10 – The Best Man	132
Chapter 11 – The Ancient Way	152
Chapter 12 – Heritage of Hope	172
Chapter 13 – Time to Get Dressed	182
Epilogue	201
A Word from the Author	206

PREFACE

Purified is a work of God. There is no chance at all that I should be able on my own merit to write something so full of God's Word and so powerful as this book. It was deposited to me in a way I can't describe as anything less than revelation and inspiration. This doesn't in any way stand as a claim for inerrancy, as I am a jar of clay complete with cracks in all the wrong places. Doubtless my role in the process has muddled what God wished to communicate through the work.

Still, the result of God's partnership with me is a piece of literature that I know contains His heart for His people in our time. When you read this, read it as though God were speaking to you. I have not tried to give you opinions on interesting subjects. I have tried to my utmost to bequeath to you the warnings and promises of God found in His Word that apply to His people in the Western world at this moment in history.

As you begin, please don't treat the book as something to "breeze through" or "skim." I *have* written it to be accessible and easy to read (I hope) to all readers, so it should flow well enough, but the points made are weighty and worthy of deep consideration. In all reality, this is a piece of devotional literature, but it is not laid out in a daily devotional format*, because it is also a body of truth that needs to be conveyed in totality in order for the full message to be received. Go slowly, listening and asking God questions, as though He were speaking to you. Consider reading this (or rereading it) in times of quiet prayer before God with an open Bible. If you want to gain the fruit I believe God intended this work to produce, then you need to take some time with it. Think of it like courtship. You need to get to know God better, and this book can help you do that, but it takes time. Love ought not to be rushed.

As you contemplate diving into *Purified*, you might want to know what to expect. Let's begin with some verses from Isaiah 1, where we'll find God's heart in commissioning the writing of this book:

> "'What to me is the multitude of your sacrifices?' says the Lord; '**I have had enough** of burnt offerings of rams and the fat of well-fed beasts; I do not delight in the blood of bulls, or of lambs, or of goats. When you come to appear before me, who has required of you this trampling of my courts? Bring no more vain offerings; incense is an abomination to me. New moon and Sabbath and the calling of convocations—**I cannot endure iniquity and solemn assembly.** Your new moons and your appointed feasts my soul hates; they have become a burden to me; I am weary of bearing them. **When you spread out your hands, I will hide my eyes from you; even though you make many prayers, I will not listen**; your hands are full of blood. Wash yourselves; **make yourselves clean; remove the evil of your deeds from before my eyes;** cease to do evil, learn to do good; seek justice, correct oppression; bring justice to the fatherless, plead the widow's cause. **Come now, let us reason together,'**

says the Lord: 'though your sins are like scarlet, they shall be as white as snow; though they are red like crimson, they shall become like wool. If you are willing and obedient, you shall eat the good of the land; but if you refuse and rebel, you shall be eaten by the sword; for the mouth of the Lord has spoken." — Isaiah 1:12-20, ESV, emphasis mine

This passage expresses God's thoughts for His people, Israel, as they faced impending judgment for ignoring His commands. They were doing their religious duty, having events, making sacrifices, and offering prayers, but God was not remotely pleased with them. As Jesus said using some of Isaiah's words, *"These people draw near to Me with their mouth and honor Me with their lips, but their heart is far from Me. And in vain they worship Me, teaching as doctrines the commandments of men"* (Matthew 15:8-9). They were going through the motions, but their heart wasn't in it. And God deserves *more*. Because they were dishonoring God, judgment was promised if they didn't repent. As always, though, God offered hope. They could change the way they lived and change their heart towards God, and they would see their land blessed, judgment averted, and their sins forgiven.

God has been impressing on my heart for years the reality that His Church in the West (and every individual member of it) has come to a time of decision. Like ancient Israel, we must decide whether we are really committed to this covenant with God that we say we've made. He is committed to us who believe, but are we committed to Him? He is bound by love to correct us if we are not. He could cast us off, but instead, He disciplines us for our good. Are we bringing iniquity (ongoing, willful sin) to our solemn assemblies (church gatherings)? Are our mouths drawing near to God in praise while our hearts are far from Him in truth? Does He *own* us, and is that clear to the watching world? I'll tell you this: the answer had better be a firm "yes" or "no" to each of these questions. Jesus isn't interested in "maybe." He speaks in Revelation 3:15-16 to a "lukewarm" church, and His words are chilling: *"I know your works...because you are lukewarm, and neither cold nor hot, I will vomit you out of My mouth."*

Do we want to hear this from Jesus? Certainly not! But we can't expect God to keep listening to our prayers and blessing our lives when we care nothing for His kingdom. Thankfully, Jesus offers us hope a few verses later: *"I counsel you to buy from Me gold refined in the fire, that you may be rich; and white garments, that you may be clothed, that the shame of your nakedness may not be revealed; and anoint your eyes with eye salve, that you may see. As many as I love, I rebuke and chasten. Therefore, be zealous and repent"* (Revelation 3:18-19). It's time to be purified, and this book is our guide. If you will make the effort to meet with God and be changed, and if others will do the same all across the West, we will see the Church rise like the sun to give light to all in the house, and the world will see the work of our God and give Him glory on the last day.

*Note: I intend to create a daily devotional journey book (40 days, perhaps) and a small group study guide based on *Purified* if I hear back from people showing me a need, so drop me a line at www.storyreborn.com if interested.

Prologue

As the blazing brightness of the afternoon sun faded into the soft glow of velvet twilight, the stillness was broken by the merry peal of wedding bells issuing from an ages-old chapel nestled high in the Swiss Alps. The sound echoed out across the valley, filling the evening with a sense of joyful expectation.

Inside the chapel, the final vestiges of sunlight shone through stained glass, casting multicolored hues across the congregated guests and outlining the beaming face of the groom as he waited for his bride-to-be. Mahogany timber walls enclosed the gathering, framing a simple yet elegant wooden altar that the groom had built himself. He was a carpenter by trade, and it had been a labor of love. In a moment, the lilting sound of violin harmony ceased, hush filled the room, and every eye turned to the back of the chapel. The time had come.

Waiting with bated breath, the groom inhaled deeply, calming himself. She was here, and she would be his—forever. Stringed instruments started up in earnest, singing out a joyous, majestic tune, and his heart soared with the rising volume of the music. The great sanctuary doors swung open, and a procession of lovely bridesmaids stepped out first, but he only had eyes for one—and there she was. The bride had arrived.

As she slowly slipped into view, gasps of disbelief sounded throughout the chapel. One might have thought that her beauty had taken their breath away, but the astonished looks commanding nearly every face told a very different story—they were disgusted.

The young lady was nearly naked, and what clothes she did have appeared worn, unwashed, and barely covered her enough to call her dressed. Yet, she did not seem bothered in the least about her embarrassing state. Her cheeks were too proud to blush. Chin held high, she was strutting down the aisle as though she owned the place, glaring at other women, sneering at the décor as though it was beneath her, and casting sultry glances at every attractive man she passed—married or otherwise.

The whole affair was horrific, but you wouldn't have known it by looking at the groom. His eyes were fixated on his bride's face, and his accepting smile still welcomed her to the altar, though there may perhaps have been a slight sadness in his eyes. He remained the picture of joy—but he was the only one.

Nearly everyone present looked mortified, and the bride's family was growing nervous. Then there were the groom's parents. One look at his father would have made any observer painfully aware of his simmering displeasure. His face was set like a flint, fists clenched, and wrath was rising in his eyes. It didn't seem as if he would keep his silence for long.

At long last, the bride arrived at the altar. The musicians had been forced to play the bridal march twice, and it had taken so long that one wondered whether she wanted to be there at all. Even inches away, she still wouldn't look the groom in the eye. Yet, she seemed resigned to her fate against her better judgment.

The groom reached out and took her by the hands, pulling her close and clearly striving to break through her cold façade. She only gave a hurried nod to his whispered attempts to connect with her, obviously ready to get the event over with. And that was the last straw.

Thud! The father of the groom slammed his fist into the wooden pew and rose from his seat. His son was *not* going to marry this girl—not like this. "No!" he shouted, baritone voice reverberating painfully through the quiet chapel. The groom's head turned, confusion and disappointment etched on his features. This was not what this day was supposed to be.

The father grabbed his son by the shoulders, turning him away from his bride. Looking in the young man's eyes, he pleaded, "Please, don't marry her, my son." Then his gaze turned to his would-be daughter-in-law, eyes aflame. "And *you*." He was visibly shaking, clearly struggling to remain composed. "You should be ashamed of yourself. We have welcomed you as a member of this family, and this is how you treat my only son?" He shook his head in disgust. "I don't even know what to say to you." Her glazed and clearly unrepentant look didn't help.

He might have continued, but the feel of his son's soft touch on his shoulder interrupted his tirade. "Father, she is the one. She is to be my wife." The groom spoke quietly but firmly, confident in his conviction. His father looked back at him, tears welling up in his eyes, and compassion filled his heart. *How he loved her.* But what could be done?

The father turned slowly back to the bride before addressing her sternly but kindly for his son's sake. Still, the tone of his voice left no room for argument. "My son deserves a beautiful, faithful, devoted bride. I want you to march back out of this chapel and take some time to prepare yourself for him properly. Search your heart, get yourself in order, and come back with a nice, modest dress, a changed attitude, and eyes reserved for my son. Then, maybe we can have a real wedding, and you can join this family. Then, and only then, may you have my blessing."

He turned his back on her, appearing to be finished with the conversation—and possibly finished with the young lady for good—but he only beckoned one of the bridesmaids to come to him with some small object. Upon receiving it, he turned to face the bride once again, looking her squarely in the eyes in a way that stayed any attempts at evasion. He held up a small, simple wooden mirror. "Take a long, hard look at yourself. See what you have become."

She hesitated, uncertain whether she wanted such a gift, but his stern visage warranted only one response, so she took it begrudgingly. He held up a finger. "If you are willing to see it, this mirror will show you the truth about yourself. It will reveal to you what needs to be changed. See, truly see, and take note." His eyes softened as he spoke once again. "But after that, I want you to look at my son, *really look at him*. Look into his eyes and see what He sees. See the person He intends to marry, the person you are meant to be. See the kindness in His gaze. See the depths of His love for you."

He then went to stand closer to his son, grasping him by the arm. "If, after that, you are able to enter this place with a heart full of love for Him and an appearance reflecting that heart, then we will have a wedding." He then frowned decisively, finishing, "And if not, then you have no place in this family. **See to it that you make the right choice.**"

Chapter 1

Remembering Our Anniversary

*"As you therefore have received Christ Jesus the
Lord, so walk in Him."*
— Colossians 2:6

HAVE YOU BEEN FAITHFUL TO JESUS? Don't be too hasty to answer. You'll have the entire length of this book to mull it over and meet with God on the subject. And let me be clear, you *must* meet with Him, discerning the answer in the quiet place of prayer where God can really speak to you. No mere exercise of the mind and will can move you even an inch towards this all-important truth. It is spiritually discerned. For you, and for me, this question is one of the most pressing concerns we will face in our entire lives, so it's well worth the effort. To help us get started on the journey, let's look at a story about King David.

As many readers may know, David was hardly a saint in the "good moral example for the kids" sense. Like many people depicted in the Bible and like all of us, he was a pretty pitiful picture of humanity more often than not. He killed plenty of people, had lots of wives and mistresses, and at one point even went so far as to steal another man's wife, impregnate her, and send the fellow off to die in order to cover up his mistake. To his credit, David was eventually really sorry about the whole event and committed himself to changing his ways and living a better life—but not until he was confronted with his sin.

In 2 Samuel 12, several months after David discovered that the woman he went after (Bathsheba) was pregnant and some time after he had her husband (Uriah) "accidentally" killed, it was time for the baby to arrive. From what the Bible shares up to this point, the king appears to be unrepentant and glad to have a new wife and son, but he soon receives a visitor with an important message.

Nathan the prophet arrives to share a simple story where a rich man steals a lamb from a poor man in order to feed a traveler who stops at his home. Though the rich man had plenty of lambs he could slaughter to feed the traveler, he was self-indulgent to the point that anyone else could suffer as long as his desires were satisfied. After hearing the story, David was livid, promising to find and kill the rich man after forcing him to pay the poor man back.

To the king's surprise, Nathan pointed his finger at David, crying, "*You* are the man!" What followed was an intense but just judgment leveled against David's household. God told David that he would be embarrassed by the whole kingdom seeing someone sleep with *his* wives, his descendants would suffer violence because of the violence he leveled against Uriah, and his new son born from the unholy union would die as well. You might think that someone as selfish as David had shown himself to be would ignore Nathan or put him to death to hush him up, but the king instead demonstrated one of the many reasons he is known as a man after God's own heart. He humbled himself in repentance, recognizing the pitiful state of his soul and asking God for mercy to change. The Psalms testify to this. Many of the mournful verses filling their pages revolve around David's woeful state after having his sin uncovered and his passionate cries to God for forgiveness and a changed heart.

With all that being said, David's son still died. The other judgments also came to pass as God had spoken. His repentance did not change the consequences that his sin had wrought. What's more, David had to change the way he was living to avoid future judgments, and he doubtless had to work to repair the rift in his relationship with God. We can expect the same to be true for us. But he had God's forgiveness, and God's presence returned to his life. And that was *everything*.

Now, after a story like that, many of us probably feel a bit like David did about the rich man in the story. We're tempted to sneer at David's evil deeds thinking of how *we* would never make a choice like *that*. But in that moment, Jesus's words are a warning to us, *"Judge not, that you be not judged. For with what judgment you judge, you will be judged; and with the measure you use, it will be measured back to you"* (Matthew 7:2), and Paul's admonishment begins to be fulfilled in us: *"Therefore you are inexcusable, O man, whoever you are who judge, for in whatever you judge another you condemn yourself; for you who judge practice the same things"* (Romans 2:1).

If you take offense at this, take a second look with me at the introduction of this book. How much do you resemble the bride in the story? Are you looking forward to the day you will be united with Jesus Christ, the Lover of your soul? Are you even looking at Him now, living a life aimed at the altar? Or are you distracted by the décor, the things you see around you that have nothing to do with Him and your life together? Do you find your eyes wandering across the aisle to other suitors (people or pursuits that you feel have more to offer you) or to your competition (other Christians)? Do heaven and the idea of the marriage feast only matter to you because they make a good end to your story? Or does the thought of an occasion entirely devoted to celebrating the Son of God bring you inexpressible joy because of how deeply your heart knows *He deserves it* for who He is—and you are honored just to be part of it?

I don't know about you, but I'm ashamed of my answers to some of these questions. I do not live a life each day that reflects the depth of pure devotion that I am confident Jesus Christ deserves for the way He has loved me. But I want to. I dearly want to. As the Word says, *"Blessed are the pure in heart, for they shall see God"* (Matthew 5:8). I get to *see* God and be overwhelmed with joy if my heart is "pure." The word means "unmixed with any other thing" or "untainted," and we use it to show value. We say an object is "pure gold," so that others can be confident there are no other metals involved in the making of the object, and this increases its value in our eyes. To be a *pure* bride is to be a bride that has not been tainted by intimacy with other lovers. Such a bride only has eyes for her groom, and she only shares herself with him. For all of us, what God wants to see and what the world needs to see is a people being conformed to His image that display *His own character* on the earth. God's people are meant to be "pure Jesus," a people who do not mix with the world or any lesser substance than divinity. We should worship with pure devotion, a singular desire for God above all else. And like the groom's father in the Prologue parable, God is committed to helping us see ourselves honestly—as David at last saw himself in the light of Nathan's parable—and be changed into a pure bride worthy of our

Lord. He simply waits for us to look in the mirror of His Word (James 1:22-25), fix our eyes on the love of His Son (2 Cor. 3:18), and make a commitment to Him that will last from now into eternity (John 17:3).

Back To The Cross

When I met Jesus, I was a lonely youth, the sort that kept to himself to stay safe from failure. Growing up, my family had not often been involved in regular church attendance, but I had been on enough occasions with my mother or grandparents that the Gospel had been shared with me a number of times. I knew about Jesus and what He had done on the cross, and I knew that if ever I needed help, He would be there. But I had to reach a place where I was desperate for rescue. One day, I finally was.

I was just beginning to drive and work my first job when it started—the deep, indescribable angst of an unfulfilled soul. Most will know what I am talking about. I just knew that I was not happy with what my life was or where it was going, and I began to get a very mature sense that the road I was on would not end well. I was already nearly completely devoid of self-control, spending countless hours and all of my waking thoughts focused on a number of addictions, and I was unmotivated to succeed in work or education beyond what it took to maintain an acceptable reputation so I could be left to my habits.

It was in that dark night of the soul that Jesus entered in as the light of the world. To this day, I am confident God had been in hot pursuit of my life since my childhood. He does that for us, you know. Like a mysterious lover longing to woo his lady at any cost, God entreats us with joys and favor, protects us from hidden dangers, and asks us time and again for our attention. He does not do this because of any need in Himself, but out of the genuine passion of a soul that *is* love. He can do no other.

So it was that He pursued me, and I at last gave Him my hand in covenant partnership. I was alone at my computer, committed to doing no good for the duration of the night and morning, when my heart was overwhelmed with grief at the state of my life. I was hit with a barrage of thoughts and feelings as my imagination played through the next decades of living for myself, and I had a glimpse of a terrible, unknown, and pointless end to the life I was building. In that moment, God revived the seeds of the Gospel that had been scattered onto the tainted soil of my soul, and it came to me. Jesus Christ was the way out. He could rescue *anyone* from *anything*, because He had paid for sin and overcome death by resurrection. He was alive and ready to set men free, and His hand was held out to *me*.

And I took it. I agreed. I agreed with the truth about Jesus and all that He had done. I agreed that He was the King of the world and of my life, that the giving of His life purchased my life from death and the grave, and that by choosing Him I was choosing to put to death an old life in order to receive a new one. I agreed that

I no longer had any rights to my soul, because my life would now become an extension of His, a resurrected life with tremendous purpose in exchange for a pointless life with a quick and horrible end. I agreed to give Him myself to receive freedom and purpose by His side and in His arms. And for years since He has been faithful to uphold His end of that covenant, the new covenant in Jesus's blood. The question is, would I uphold mine? A day would come when God would face me with that question.

Our Lord poses the same question to us all: will we keep our vows to Him? Consider Colossians 2:6: *"As you have received Christ Jesus the Lord, so walk in Him..."* I understand this Scripture as an admonishment to go back to the beginning, to the frame of mind that allowed us to receive Christ. I believe it urges saints who have known Jesus for quite some time to revisit the day of their salvation. Now, you may not remember specifically when that was, but you should be aware of a point in time when you moved from death to life, when you went from being *aware* of *a* God to being in communion with *the* God of the Bible. After all, how many married people would say that they don't really remember getting married? They might forget the specific date of the anniversary, but you can bet everything you've got that they remember going from single to married. That's something no one forgets. Another person invades your life and you theirs. This is all the more impactful when that person is God.

So go back. Go back to the time when you were overwhelmed

and humbled in the presence of the God of the universe as you considered the awe-inspiring consequences of His Son coming to earth and facing your judgment to reunite you with Himself. Go back to the moment when you discovered what hope was, when there was suddenly something good in an otherwise grey, dead world. *And stay there.* Stay there, at the foot of the cross. Stay there, aware of your need, your desperate inability to do anything good, to offer anything back to God for all He has done. Stay in that place of desperate thankfulness where you would take anything at all from God's hand so long as He would extend it to *you*, pitiful, wicked you. *That* is what our Father wants when His Word says, *"as you received Christ Jesus the Lord, so walk in Him."* He wants every step we take in life to be taken with the cross behind and the empty tomb ahead.

Now, where does that leave you two? You and God. Do you live at the foot of the cross? Or are you in danger—as many have been, as I have been—of being so nearsighted that you are blind, having forgotten that you were cleansed from your former sins (2 Peter 1:9)? Has your anniversary with Jesus become so lost in the hustle and bustle of daily life and your "more pressing concerns" that it no longer commands the direction of your life? If this is even partly true for you, as it is for me, then you owe it to your King to spend the time you take reading this book (and every day after) to *change*.

PRAYER RESPONSE

"Father, thank you for choosing me, for being completely committed to me despite my unfaithfulness. Please forgive me for ignoring you in the press of life's concerns. You are life itself, and I have been wrong to neglect you. Help me to remember. Open my eyes to your grace that first captured my heart in the beginning of our days together. Let your Word come true in me, that as I received you, Jesus, my Lord, I might walk in you. Remind my soul of how you cast my sins as far as the east is from the west. Awaken my heart that I might love you well. I need you, Jesus, to keep my eyes fixed on the cross, because I can do no good apart from you. Please commit my heart to seeking your face during my reading of this book, and purify my soul by obedience to the truth."

— This is an example prayer from a heart touched by God's Word in the chapter. You may pray these words just as they are or let them inspire your heart to speak your own words to God. Continue daily until He answers. —

Chapter 2

Keeping Our Vows

"I will sacrifice to You with the voice of thanksgiving; I will pay what I have vowed."
— Jonah 2:9

TODAY, GOD IS LOOKING FOR YOUR HEART. He wants it all, the *whole thing*, your affection, dreams, thoughts, personality, commitment—*all of it*. He wants you, and He will not stop pursuit until He gets all of you, but He won't force you. He wants a bride who has freely and joyfully chosen to respond to her groom's dedicated pursuits. Hear His heart from Jeremiah 2:2 (ESV): "I remember the devotion of your youth, your love as a bride, how you followed me in the wilderness, in a land not sown." He longs for the days when we didn't care how much money we had or how safe the path ahead was, when we were willing to go with Him wherever He thought to go simply because *He* would be there. He wants us to believe He is enough. But He knows our weakness, that we are like a confused, adulterous woman being abused by other lovers while she has a faithful man waiting for her at home. We just need to recognize where we are and what we are missing, and *repent*. We need to remember our vows.

> "I, _____, take you, _____, to be my wedded spouse, to have and to hold, from this day forward, for better, for worse, for richer, for poorer, in sickness and in health, to love and to cherish, to honor and obey, till death do us part..."

Read slowly through the words of these traditional Protestant wedding vows. Consider Jesus, the faithful Bridegroom. Has He taken you to be His own? Has He stayed with you through thick and thin, in every phase of life? Has He cherished you and honored you above what you deserve? Will He ever leave? Even beyond death He promises to hold us. What about you? Can you say these words to Jesus and mean them wholeheartedly? Perhaps try that in prayer now. If you have made a commitment to Christ, this will tug at your heart.

Now, I doubt most of us offered these specific vows to our Lord when we met Him and chose to follow Him. But if we believe, then we promised something to Him on the day we trusted the Gospel, even if we don't remember saying so. I know that in my own life I made a very specific commitment to Christ when I accepted His hand in covenant friendship and lordship. I said, "I will do *whatever* you want me to do, if you will set me free from the things that enslave me and give my life purpose." And I meant it. I didn't know exactly *what* my words meant, because God's thoughts are as high above mine as the heavens are above the earth, but I meant what I said to Him. And He called me on it.

Just this past year (as of this writing), through a series of sovereign events—sermons heard at just the right time, friends in Christ speaking particular things over my life, signs (literal ones) on the road while praying, and the gentle tug of the Holy Spirit's still small voice in the quiet—I heard God say to me, "Remember your vows." In a climactic moment of intimate prayer, the Lord brought me to my knees both literally and in spirit. The Spirit reminded me of the story of Jonah, how he ran from God's call on his life for as long as he could until he was broken and spent, and how he met God in the belly of the great fish to answer for his unfaithfulness. His words of surrender stand as the opening of this chapter: "I *will* pay what I have vowed." God then turned the question to me. Would I keep the vow I had made to Him?

I had said He could do anything at all with my life if He gave me purpose and freedom, and He did what He'd promised, but I was withholding myself from Him. He'd asked me to preach His Word, and I had told Him no. "No, Jesus, I won't publicly proclaim your glory and goodness so that others might hear and turn towards you in faith. Yes, I know you saved me from a life of destructive and pointless selfishness and bought me with the price of your own life, but that's just too much to ask. I can't do it." Without so many words, I was standing before God with that testimony on my spiritual lips. And here He was reminding me that I had promised Him more. I could not control my weeping. Needless to say, my heart changed in the face of the overwhelming devotion of my Savior, and I am on the road to paying what I vowed during our betrothal.

That was a vow made by my own initiative in response to God's grace. You might not have made the same sort of verbal commitment when you came to Christ, and that's alright. God asks for complete belief in His Son and His finished work. That's it. But you still made a *very* clear commitment, even if you didn't fully understand its implications either. The Gospel is Good News of a new covenant, and a covenant is an agreement. Since we who are baptized into the Body of Jesus become the bride of Christ, this new covenant is our marriage contract. So what is this new covenant? What did we vow to Jesus, and He to us?

The simple answer should offer you relief beyond words and conviction beyond belief, but let's take a moment to understand the old covenant and what Jesus has done to change the terms so that this marriage survives.

Even Unto Death

"...the LORD made a covenant with Abram, saying, 'To your descendants I have given this land'" (Genesis 15:18). Though not the first agreement between God and man, Abram's covenant with God is in many ways where the old covenant of the law under Moses began, because God took His promise to Abram and later fulfilled it to His descendants who were given the land along with more, greater promises.

In the ancient world, a covenant was a binding agreement on pain of death, typically one which joined two individuals, families, or nations in intimate union. A covenant often brought the expectation that all that belonged to either party now belonged to the other. So when God came to Abram as recorded in Genesis 15, the man should have had very specific cultural expectations for covenant agreements. God told Abram to bring some animals for sacrifice, and Abram went ahead and did what was customary and cut the larger animals in half so that he and a covenant partner could walk through the pieces in symbolism of walking a path together bound in blood. Then, when Abram should have expected to meet with God and walk through the pieces as a demonstration of their mutual agreement to uphold their respective ends of the bargain on pain of death, God instead put the man to sleep. And He did it alone.

He provided a manifestation of His presence—a smoking oven and a burning torch (notably *two* parties)—and passed through the trail of blood on His own, demonstrating that He alone would keep this covenant. Already, God recognized Abram's inability to uphold his end of any potential covenant, and He displayed a beautiful foreshadowing of what He intended to do one day for all who would believe. Abram's identity was changed to Abraham by God who had lawful rights to the man's life, and God pronounced him righteous by faith alone: *"And he believed in the Lord, and He accounted it to him for righteousness"* (Genesis 15:6).

A few hundred years down the road, we see Abraham's descendants walking with God out of Egypt into the desert to follow Him to the land that He promised to their fathers. As it was spoken of in Jeremiah 2:2, God's people followed Him like a bride in the wilderness to a land not sown. In that time of betrothal, God lead Israel out into the wilderness to a mountain where He intended to have a heart-to-heart talk that would define the relationship moving forward. In this, He made a covenant with them that extended the Abrahamic Covenant, becoming what we know of today as the Old Covenant.

> *"And Moses went up to God, and the Lord called to him from the mountain, saying, "Thus you shall say to the house of Jacob, and tell the children of Israel: 'You have seen what I did to the Egyptians, and how I bore you on eagles' wings and brought you to Myself. Now therefore, if you will indeed obey My voice*

and keep My covenant, then you shall be a special treasure to Me above all people; for all the earth is Mine. And you shall be to Me a kingdom of priests and a holy nation.' These are the words which you shall speak to the children of Israel." — Ex. 19:3-6

God reminded the people of His efforts to pursue and rescue them, letting them know that this wasn't the end of the story. He had *more* in store. He wanted them to be *His* people, to belong to Him, and He would call them a special treasure above all others. That sounds like the sort of thing a man tells a woman he intends to marry, doesn't it? "Honey, you mean more to me than any other girl in the world. I only see you. Would you be mine?" God feels this way about His bride-to-be, but He also expects commitment, and He had a way that He expected Israel to show it. They were to obey His voice and keep His covenant.

Most readers are probably familiar with the ten commandments, things like "have no other gods before me," and "do not murder," which serve as key examples of what God expects of His people in this covenant. Those commandments serve in many ways as the terms of the marriage contract between God and His people—and they are not unreasonable. No one wants a spouse who is devoted to other people more than their spouse, who kills people, steals from people, and eyeballs their neighbor's property. And people can say what they like here, but at the heart level every person expects very specific things from a marriage commitment. They expect devotion, and they expect their spouse to be a certain kind of person. And that's *good*.

When you look at it the right way, there is nothing wrong with what God is doing here. He sets reasonable expectations for the relationship with his lady while promising her the world. The problem is: she's a liar. The people stand united and proclaim that they will keep the covenant, but they won't. In fact, they *can't*. The real issue is their nature. People are not, by nature, faithful. They were intended to be by God in the beginning, but when sin entered the picture, they became corrupt and untrustworthy and unable to do selfless good by their own volition. Anyone who has had a romantic relationship for very long will realize the truth of this, that their significant other is never quite selfless enough, never *just* looking out for the ones they love with no regard for themselves. They never quite do all they promised to do or what they were expected to do. And God knows this. So why the terms?

Knowing someone might fail you doesn't mean you don't let them try, right? The reality is, God knows his bride-to-be won't measure up, but the agreement is right: a good marriage *would* be built on terms like the ones He sets forth, and He loves her enough to give her a chance. He is willing to *try*, and as we see later down the road, to forgive and let her try again—and again, and again. Our capacity as humans for failure and faithlessness is unlimited, but so is God's capacity for love and faithfulness. These parts of His character stretch as far beyond our understanding of them as heaven stretches high above the earth.

So they try. And the long story short is that Israel proves to be a terrible, adulterous bride that is unwilling and unable (when occasionally willing) to keep her end of the covenant. But love finds a way. God *makes* a way.

A New Marriage Contract

Enter Jesus and the *New* Covenant. God wasn't willing to let the marriage fail. He was too invested. He cared too much about the bride. So He came to earth to get her and bring her to Himself. The problem is, she was still unfaithful and unable to join Him where He was, in a place of holiness where perfect loving commitment is the standard. So God went a step further, and He *changed the terms*, but not the terms of their faithful union, no; He changed the terms on *who* is responsible for keeping the commitments they had made. Instead of allowing His people to try and keep their own end of the agreement, He took their place and fulfilled it for them, as Jesus said, *"Do not think that I came to destroy the Law or the Prophets. I did not come to destroy but to fulfill. For assuredly, I say to you, till heaven and earth pass away, one jot or one tittle will by no means pass from the law till all is fulfilled"* (Matthew 5:17-18).

The covenant terms were right. They were *good*. So God made a way to take care of them for us. Jesus, God the Son, lived a perfect life as a faithful covenant partner with God the Father, being fully obedient in every way. Then, He had to deal with the consequences of the bride's unfaithfulness. She was due death for her adultery, and He loved her too much to allow this, so He stood in her place, accepting the cruel death of the cross and the just wrath of God for her constant sinful living. And at last, He rose from death to become her faithful groom forever, the one who always lives to stand for her, the one who will be there with her always to the end of time and into eternity. And if any person will come to God with a heart fully trusting in the true character of Jesus and His finished work on their behalf, they will become a part of His bride and be united with Him always in beautiful covenant partnership, despite all they've done to deserve less. What a *relief*.

Now there is a new covenant. At the last supper, during Passover, just before Jesus went to die for His people, He took a cup of wine and said to them, *"This cup is the new covenant in My blood, which is shed for you"* (Luke 22:20). As the Old Covenant was inaugurated by the blood of bulls and goats, and as God passed through the trail of blood for Abraham's sake, now the New Covenant would be made in the blood of Jesus. If either God or His people broke this covenant, it would be Jesus's blood that would be spilled. Jesus spoke of this New Covenant during Passover, a poignant reminder that God had sent wrath upon all of Egypt but preserved every one of His own people who put the blood of an innocent lamb on their doorpost. He passed over their sins because a sacrifice had already been made. So it is that

Jesus entered into union with His bride promising the protection of His own blood to cover their sins so that God's wrath can pass over them when they break the terms of the covenant.

God wrote and fulfills a marriage contract that is essentially unbreakable for the one who would choose to join Him in covenant partnership. *He* promises to keep *our* vows as well as His own. Who could ask for more? And in response, He expects love—freely given love.

When a man pursues a woman with genuinely pure intentions, desiring to love and serve her for the rest of his days in intimate union, he does not *demand* but naturally *expects* love in return. It's not payment due. It's a beautiful and natural response to love freely given. Most people can recognize that, but it's important to point out, because people think that God's desire is different. The reality is, our lesser love for one another is only an image of the greater love into which He invites us. God *is* love (1 John 4:8), among many other things, *"and everyone who loves is born of God and knows God"* (1 John 4:7).

So when Jesus calls any one of us to unite with Him in covenant, He says, *"If anyone loves Me, he will keep My word; and My Father will love him, and We will come to him and make Our home with him. He who does not love Me does not keep My words..."* (John 14:23-24). Jesus loves us before we have ever done *anything* to love Him in return. But here He draws a line in the sand. Here, He helps us understand that such great love *will* produce a response in anyone who truly cares for Him. You can't join the body and bride of Christ if you don't love Him. You wouldn't marry someone you didn't love unless you were forced to, and God is not in the business of forcing love. We all know what that is called.

And the love described here is *not* just a feeling that you feel some days and not others, especially when we are considering Jesus. God gets to define love, because it comes from Him and belongs to Him, and we should all recognize real love when we see it. Jesus shares what genuine love towards Him looks like: obedience. Think back to the wedding vows shared earlier in the chapter, vows you may well have spoken to another in the past: "to honor and obey…" Obedience is part of love. It involves freely submitting our will to another, one of the most intimate of acts, because of the tremendous trust required. To let my life be guided by the intentions of another, I must trust them *completely*—or else feel used and abused.

If you love Jesus, you *will* desire to obey Him. If your love has grown cold, you owe it to Him to pursue Him until it is revived again, or else to discover a love that has perhaps never truly been there in your heart. Obedience is the vow that we all make to Jesus when we come to Him for salvation. Obedience is what Jesus deserves for what He has done for us. We should see His perfect character and the awe-inspiring overflow of His love for us as expressed through His personal suffering and sacrifice on our behalf, and we should *respond*. Nothing less is acceptable, and nothing less should assure us that we are a part of His bride. There is a reason that God says to be diligent to make our calling and election sure (2 Peter 1:10). Our love for Jesus as expressed through an obedient life is the true confirmation of our being a part of His true bride. His true bride loves Him, and she obeys, and she has *joy* in the process—not always, perhaps, but it *must* be there.

So the question that the Word of God lays before us is this: Will we keep our vows? When Jesus asks us to suffer with Him for His Name's sake, will we do it? When He tells us that our love for others is proof of our love for Him, can we do anything else but change the way we treat people made in His image? When He shares with us the things that He cares about: truth, unconditional love, the orphan, the sick, the weak, the wayward, the widow, His *glory*, can we do ought else but strive to turn our hearts and entire lives towards caring about the same things? Is this a real marriage or not? Do we want to *know* Him and be known by Him, or not? Choose this day whom you will love. As for me and my house, we will love the Lord.

Prayer Response

"Jesus, from day one, I was always going to fail you. You knew that, and you *still* loved me. You still chose *me*. Thank you for not only rescuing me from myself, but for making a covenant I can't break. Because you have kept your covenant with the Father as a perfect man, I know you can keep mine for me. So I want to serve you, not to pay you back, but because I love you. I want to show you my love the way you've asked me to, by obedience. I recognize that in receiving salvation I made a vow to obey you and to cherish you. So grant me the strength of soul to do whatever you say, whenever you say it. Give me a thirst for your Word and make my desire for you grow. Teach my heart you are enough for me."

Also try the prayer below to remind yourself of the commitment you made when you said, "I'm a Christian."

"I, _____, take you, Jesus, to be my faithful Bridgeroom, to have and to hold, from this day forward, for better, for worse, for richer, for poorer, in sickness and in health, to love and to cherish, to honor and obey, till death unites us always."

Chapter 3

The Groom

"When I found the one I love, I held him and would not let him go."
— Song of Solomon 3:4

WHEN WAS THE LAST TIME YOU FOUND JESUS? How did you find Him? What was He like? In Song of Solomon, perhaps the most romantic book in the Bible, much of the book is given to the Shulamite bride's effusive praise of her bridegroom, Solomon. She sings and shouts and weeps over her desire for the one she loves and the worthiness of his character. He is strong, handsome, and brave. Thoughts of him fill every waking moment, and she can't live without him. We all recognize the beauty and intrigue of romance. This is part of love, the attraction of one person to the personhood of another, to *who they are*. We wouldn't even speak of someone as attractive if we could not know them or at least see them. So it is with Jesus.

Jesus. Yeshua. Adonai. Faithful Bridegroom. Wonderful Counselor. Provider. Healer. Mighty God. King of Kings. I could go on and on. In the bible, names carry with them something of the nature of a person. They're *very* important. So when we see that God has names upon names in the Bible, we realize that each showcases something of his infinite character. Each revealed name shares yet another part of the unfathomable depths of God's precious personhood. And as He is revealed, He can be known. In knowing Him, we will find that we are attracted to Him. As a man in love finds himself shouting to the rooftops that the woman he desires is better than life, so any person who truly finds Jesus as He is will be overcome with loving adoration. The difference is, this union is what we were made for; to Jesus alone can the iconic words, "you complete me," be truly and honestly spoken. He *is* life, joy, peace, comfort, and love.

Jesus told us, *"...this is eternal life, that they may know You, the only true God, and Jesus Christ whom You have sent"* (John 17:3). Knowing God is life. This isn't just about getting to heaven where you'll never die, either. All that "living" consists of—starting now and continuing forever after the grave—is bound up in becoming acquainted with God. This "knowing" is the same knowing that

Adam and Eve experienced when they consummated their union in the garden of Eden: *complete* knowledge of another. But with God it is yet deeper. Physical union brings limited intimacy, as anyone experiencing marriage will know. There is a deeper union at the level of the soul that people rarely reach and are not often able to touch for more than a moment. In that place, the realm of the spirit, true personhood resides. And God *is* Spirit. Knowing God happens at the deepest place of human being, and it is no casual relationship. It takes complete trust and vulnerability, passionate pursuit, and a malleable soul. God's desire is to meet with us, *see* us in all our insecurity, beauty, and struggle, and reveal Himself to us until we are overcome with attraction to Him—until we are mastered by love. And loving God changes us. It makes us *more*, because if our Groom is anything, He is infinitely more than anything and everything else we have ever known.

What Love Is

So do you know Him? Don't take it as a chance to check the "Christian" box. "Yes sir, Mr. Evangelist, we are good. I know Jesus. Not to worry. You can go find somebody else to give your fire insurance." If we consider ourselves Christians, it's easy to have this kind of reaction to the question. But the reality is, Jesus is so magnificent that our devotion to Him should drive us to ecstasy when we hear His Name. Being asked if we know Jesus should invoke in us a cry of passion, "YES, but barely. I long to know Him more! Please, tell me more." The sad fact is we often accept a surface understanding of Jesus that comes nowhere near the totality of His person, and we become familiar with *that* idea of Him to a point that borders on contempt. "Oh, Jesus, yes. Yes, I know." God *forbid!* How dare we treat the lover of our soul with such disdain?

Just Jesus? *"He is the image of the invisible God, the firstborn over all creation..."* (Colossians 1:15). He was first. He is first, and He is last, the beginning of all things and the end of all things: *"He is before all things, and in Him all things consist"* (Colossians 1:17). Nothing matters more than Him. The universe revolves around Him and is *"upheld by the word of His power,"* (Hebrews 1:3). He made you. In fact, all things were created through Him and for Him (Colossians 1:16). When you consider the great purpose for which you are made, do you consider that it is Jesus's pleasure? However you came to be, through whomever parents, and at whatever point in history, you were made for Him. This is not just a God who wants to know you, this is one who has "fashioned your heart" (Psalm 33:15). He knows every deep, personal desire that He has placed in your soul and every perversion that you've allowed to corrupt it. He is also the one who loved you when you were committing adultery with everyone and everything in your world beside Him.

As the prophet Hosea continued to take his wife back after she chose again and again to run after other lovers, so Jesus has taken you back time after time no matter how heart-wrenching your failure to honor and respect Him has been. Jesus is faithful. *"If we are faithless, He remains faithful. He cannot deny Himself"* (2 Timothy 2:13). He takes His bride to be His own—to be one with Him—and He loves her as His own Body. *"Husbands ought to love their own wives as their own bodies; he who loves his wife loves himself. For no one ever hated his own flesh, but nourishes and cherishes it, just as the Lord does the church. For we are members of His body, of His flesh and of His bones"* (Ephesians 5:28-29). Jesus demonstrated this in a way that no other man has ever been able to do since. He allowed Himself to be made guilty in her place, and He chose to be judged and punished for her adultery. What a man!

Now you and I both know that Jesus is good, and we'd accept any amount of praise aimed His way without question, but we have to ask if we are *in love* with Him. Do you find it hard to take your eyes off of Him long enough to do daily tasks? Or are you much more like the bride-to-be in the opening parable of this book, eyes wandering to and fro looking for something to satisfy, but without one glance in every dozen towards your bridegroom? We are *supposed* to love Jesus for who He is. We hear about His glory and His grace and the praise He deserves, we say "Hallelujah" when the preacher asks for it, and we clap for Jesus and stand up for Jesus—we even feel a little guilty when the pastor tells us we ought to do more for Jesus—but do we *love* Him?

How do you know? The Bible gives us a good answer on this

one, one that all of us can understand if we've lived very long. We can see it by watching Jesus. Remember, Jesus is our example, that we should follow in His steps (1 Peter 2:21). What does the man Jesus do as often as He can get the chance? Heal the sick? Sure. Put corrupt religious leaders in their place? Absolutely, on occasion. Teach the truth? Probably just about every day. But what does He deliberately leave all these other activities to do on a regular basis? What does His heart appear to yearn for so much that He would stop rescuing souls to do it? Read Luke 5:16: *"He Himself often withdrew into the wilderness and prayed."* He went to be with His Father. He went to be with the one He loved.

The love within the Trinity is perfect, the source from which all other love flows. Jesus spoke of this at the last supper before He sacrificed Himself. He said to His followers, *"As the Father loved Me, I also have loved you; abide in My love. If you keep My commandments, you will abide in My love, just as I have kept My Father's commandments and abide in His love...Father, I desire that they also whom You gave Me may be with Me where I am, that they may behold My glory which You have given Me; for You loved Me before the foundation of the world"* (John 15:9-10, John 17:24). Jesus experienced such love before He came to earth that He longed to return to be with His Father more than anything else He experienced while He was here. That's what love is like. Love means you're more attracted to the object of your love than anything else in your vision. Jesus understood that, and He calls us to love Him in the same way.

Even the Bible's admonitions on things to avoid demonstrate the power of love. What does old Apostle John tell the wayward children of the church? *"Do not love the world or the things in the world. If anyone loves the world, the love of the Father is not in him"* (1 John 2:15). You see, John is warning the church to watch their heart to see what it *yearns* after, what it *pursues*. If they love the world, they go after it because they are attracted to it. He calls them instead to go after God as God has gone after them. Knowing this is one thing, but how do we do it? How do we change what we love? *"With men this is impossible, but with God all things are possible"* (Matthew 19:26). *"You do not have because you do not ask God"* (James 4:2). Start with asking the one who is capable of raising dead men's bones. This is where the true power to change lies.

Look to Jesus

But for our own part, we can take a lesson from living. What do we do when we want something? We look at it often, hoping to gain it. When we look at it more, our love for it seems to naturally increase. To behold the object of our desire is to grow in desire. So let us look to *Jesus*. *"We all, with unveiled face, beholding as in a mirror the glory of the Lord, are being transformed into the same image from glory to glory..."* (2 Corinthians 3:18). God is not only calling us to look at Jesus, He is promising that the very looking itself will *change* us. Jesus is *that* amazing. Reality itself melts and reshapes before Him.

This process sounds beautiful and unstoppable, doesn't it? But we have to get practical and deal with our present reality. Most of us don't *feel* like our personal reality—including our own character—is being transformed by just being near Jesus. It would seem that God has not told us the truth here, or that there is perhaps a metaphor at work. Practically, we say to ourselves, "that is nice, I should definitely spend more time with Jesus," then we move on to do *real* life because this verse feels beyond us. Maybe we get a few short minutes "with" Jesus if we set aside regular time for that through prayer and/or time reading/listening to the Bible, but if we begin to be changed into His image, it is certainly not by much, and the truth we receive is often soon forgotten or the progress we gained is lost in the press of the day's events and concerns. In the words of James from the early church, "brethren, this ought not to be so!"

And it isn't God's fault. Sure, we all know it's never God's fault, but practically, we might as well be blaming God for not keeping His Word if we don't take the blame ourselves in repentance and move forward in obedience. The honest answer is, we don't "behold" Jesus just because we read the Bible or say a prayer on a given day. Remember, Jesus's strongest rebukes during His first coming were aimed at the most religious people: the Pharisees and Sadducees. These people were the ones who read

Scripture until they were blue in the face, had memorized most of it since childhood, and even taught its truths to others on a regular basis. They also *loved* to pray, though that was mostly for show. They wanted to be seen doing the right thing (which is not so different from the reason some of us pray, at times, I think). It is to them that Jesus says, *"You search the Scriptures, for in them you think you have eternal life; and these are they which testify of Me. But you are not willing to come to Me that you may have life"* (John 5:39). No matter how much they read, they weren't meeting with Jesus, even though God's Word testifies of Him on every page.

We may say, "yes, but these were *lost* people." Sure, but they thought they knew God very well, and Jesus had come to reveal Himself to "God's people." The fact is, plenty of "church people" neglect Jesus every day, just like plenty of "Christian" husbands neglect their wives every day. This isn't supposed to happen, but it does. So what will we do about it? A man needs to remind himself what it is he loves about his wife (or discover what that is, if he has not truly loved her), and every Christian needs to remind themselves what it is they love about Jesus—every day!

We learned in Sunday School that *most* of the time, Jesus is the answer to every question. The thing is, that's not far from the truth. In the beginning of his first letter to Corinth, Paul speaks to a church that has been thinking far too much of themselves and far too little of Jesus, saying, *"...you are in Christ Jesus, who became for us wisdom from God—and righteousness and sanctification and redemption—that, as it is written, 'He who glories, let him glory in the Lord'"* (1 Corinthians 1:30-31). Paul didn't say Jesus *gave* the Corinthians wisdom or righteousness, but that He *became* those things to them. Not many of them were wise, but Jesus became wisdom to them. None was righteous, no not one, but Jesus became sin so that they might become the righteousness of God in Him. No Corinthian had redeemed themselves or been sanctified (made holy for service to God), but Jesus became that reality. To be baptized into Jesus is to become sanctified and to join the ranks of the redeemed. He is all of this and more to the Christian—and even to the lost He is more than they could dream! This is why every knee *will* bow and every tongue *will* confess that Jesus is Lord on the last day. God is not in the habit of forcing worship against people's will, but on that day each person will willingly bow and confess the name of the King of Kings. Is it not right for the children of God to endeavor to fix their eyes on this person who is everything to them? May our gaze never leave His face.

What's It to You?

So, what is it that you love about Jesus? What has He done for you? What *is* He *to* you? Is He hope? Is He healing? Is He mercy? Tell yourself again in the morning, rouse your sleeping soul with a dose of it in the evening, and give Him praise! Let *Him* know how you feel about Him! Share your love song that He might dance to it, and if it is weak or near nonexistent, sing what you wish it was until it becomes reality. After all, what is it that Jesus *isn't*? What do you find lacking in Him? If you can't answer that, then start giving Him glory for the tremendous value that must be there, even if you can't put a finger on it. If you have an answer, then let the Scriptures cast down the thoughts of this world and lift up your eyes to heaven to see that He is all you need. The Lord Himself is our portion. *He* is what we get!

Even history is about Jesus. Just parse out the word, "his-story," and you get the point. I realize that the etymology of history doesn't lead to that conclusion, but God can use *just about anything* to display His glory. In fact, until the godless "wise of this age," started trying to erase it recently with the replacement "C.E.," our designation for the years passing on calendars all around the world was about Jesus. This book was published in 2021 A.D., *Anno Domini*, a Latin phrase meaning "the year of our Lord." It's been roughly 2,021 years since Jesus was born, and the world has been measuring time's passing by that day for hundreds and hundreds of years, because *Jesus changes everything*!

This book itself has been written with the express purpose of bringing glory to Jesus. In many ways, this writing is an attempt to effect certain changes in the people of God, and I believe with all I am that God Himself desires to do a work in His people in this hour, but this is not really why the book exists. It exists for His name and His fame. The Church *must* be purified because God *must* be glorified. The world should see God when it looks at His people made in His image, baptized into His Son, and filled with His Spirit! He deserves no less.

Read Ezekiel 36:22-38, and you'll see God's heart on the matter. The first few verses read, *"Thus says the Lord God: 'It is not for your sake, O house of Israel, that I am about to act, but for the sake of my holy name, which you have profaned among the nations to which you came. And I will vindicate the holiness of my great name, which has been profaned among the nations, and which you have profaned among them. And the nations will know that I am the Lord, declares the Lord God, when through you I vindicate my holiness before their eyes.'"* God is about to purify His people. He is at work even now in you and in me. He is about to raise up the people of God in the West to a higher standard, and it is not for our sake that He is about to act—though he loves us dearly—it is for His Name's sake. The Western Church has represented God wrongly for far too long, and He will have no more of it. His mercy is new every morning, but His judgment is sure as sunrise, and it begins at the household of God (1 Peter 4:17). The world *will* know who it is that sits on the throne in heaven. They will know the King of Kings, and He will vindicate His holiness by making His people holy as He is holy.

Prayer Response

"Jesus, whatever I might really think of you in my heart, I know you are *more*. You are everything my soul wishes you could be and everything I was searching for when I wasn't searching for you. As your Word says, you sustain *all* things. You make my heart beat and fill my lungs with breath. I need you. You are the way, the truth, and the life, and I can't make it through life without you. I long to behold you. Please give my soul the strength and my eyes the sight to behold you, that I might know your love that surpasses knowledge. You said eternal life is wrapped up in knowing you. And what a wonder that you want to know me, too! I want to meet you in my struggles and share my insecurities with you so you can make me solid as a rock. Please forgive me for thinking I have given you what you deserve in the few minutes here and there we have spent together. Thank you for your faithfulness to me. You complete me."

Chapter 4

Knowledge of the Holy

"I am the Lord your God. You shall therefore consecrate yourselves, and you shall be holy; for I am holy." — Leviticus 11:44, 1 Peter 1:16

Be holy, for I am holy. What does that even mean? It's one of those statements in the Bible that many of us read and end up glossing right over because we have no idea how to take it to heart. God's holiness sets Him apart from everything else that exists. He is holy: He is completely *other*. He is more. He is beyond all things and set apart from all things at a distance no one can cross. So how can He expect us to be like Him?

When God first spoke these words to His people from the

tabernacle in the wilderness, the honest answer was: you are *not* like me, and you can't be. The Old Testament message of the law was clear. We are too sinful to engage with a holy God and attempting to draw near to Him ends in death. However, throughout the Old Testament, God also does something that mankind could never have expected. He persists in drawing near to us. Moses met with God on the mountain because God *called* him to the mountain to meet with Him. The prophets existed because God *wanted* people to hear from Him, and He established the priesthood to *allow* people to come near by the blood of sacrifice. So we have a paradox: God wants people near, but He won't allow them near as they are. This seems like an impossible situation, and it should, but *anything* is possible with God. To find the answer, we must look in the fire.

Fire is a mysterious and powerful thing. It, too, is a paradox. Being close to a fire can be a pleasant experience, or it can be our worst nightmare. A fire's heat can draw people near to be warmed by its pleasing presence, yet its intensity burns flesh and destroys cities. I can't think of many more painful ways to die than by fire, as some of our brethren experienced in ancient Rome under Emperor Nero when the tradition of the day was to light up Christians as living torches if they wouldn't bow to Caesar. But I also have never seen people come together like they do around a fire on a cold night. Something about it just makes people want to draw near. So it is with God.

Though every metaphor fails to convey the full truth of the infinite God, He acknowledges our finite understanding and has chosen to reveal Himself to us through things we recognize. When God revealed Himself to the people of Israel in the wilderness, Moses told them, *"The Lord your God is a consuming fire"* (Deuteronomy 4:24). The Lord had revealed Himself to Moses in this way at the very first, showing up in a burning bush, though the bush was, notably, *not* consumed. He demonstrated that His nature was so intense that it could destroy a lesser substance, but the intact bush also showed His ability to sustain something, preserving it from certain destruction in His presence. He changed the bush and its surroundings so that it could stand the fire, and in so doing, He made it holy. *"He said, 'Do not draw near this place. Take your sandals off your feet, for the place where you stand is holy ground'"* (Exodus 3:5).

God's fiery presence arrived in that place and *transformed* it to make it like Himself. When fire touches an object, it transforms the object into fire, and whatever can't be transformed is destroyed, leaving only ashes. In the same way, God, the Consuming Fire, either transforms a person to make them part of His fire or destroys what can't be transformed. God is Holy, and He is fire, and when the fire of His presence meets a person, that person must become holy like Him or be destroyed. This brings us back to the paradox. God spoke in the wilderness, "be holy, as I am holy," but He also said, "don't let the people draw near the mountain to touch it, lest they be destroyed."

Changed into His Likeness

And yet, God was able to set Moses apart from the rest of the people to allow Him on the mountain near His presence in the wilderness, much as He was able to set the bush apart and save it from destruction in the fire. Moses was transformed by this experience, so much so that people were overwhelmed by the change in his physical appearance, as the Word says, *"when Aaron and all the children of Israel saw Moses, behold, the skin of his face shone, and they were afraid to come near him"* (Exodus 34:30). The man Moses was so touched by being near the holiness of God that people experienced something of the fear of the Lord when they met him. He had something more of God's likeness upon him.

But it was not permanent, as Paul shares with us in the New Testament, *"But if the ministry of death, written and engraved on stones, was glorious, so that the children of Israel could not look steadily at the face of Moses because of the glory of his countenance—<u>which glory was passing away</u>—how will the ministry of the Spirit not be more glorious?"* (2 Corinthians 3:7-8, emphasis mine). As the terms stood, Moses could not be made holy permanently, and neither could the people or the priesthood. For a select few, there was a way to be made holy for a moment to atone for the sins of the people, by ceremonial washings, specific prayers, and the blood of innocent animals—*but it always ended.* They always had to do it all again.

Then Jesus came. And when He came, old, seemingly dead promises about God's people being a "holy nation," began to breathe again. The first Adam had walked away from God's holy presence in the garden to forge his own way on the earth, and it had brought nothing but death. Now the second Adam had come, a new man with a right heart, who did nothing apart from the Father and *always* did what pleased Him. Now, mankind had a representative who could go into the holy of holies in heaven, a spectacular place of which the copy in the Jewish temple was only the faintest shadow, as it is written, *"these are a shadow of things to come, but the substance is of Christ"* (Colossians 2:17).

Jesus tore the veil! He opened a way through the curtain that kept people from God's holy presence. Now, people can get to God! By grace through faith that baptizes the believing soul into the very body of Jesus, men and women all over the world are made holy. When we become part of Jesus, we become what Jesus is, and Jesus is as holy as it gets. Now, our life is hidden with Christ *in* God (Colossians 3:3). What a wonder! The perfect, resurrected Christ who is set apart from all things is now one with sinful man. But by force of His own immutably holy nature, this Christ changes the sinner into the saint by His very presence as surely as God changed the burning bush into a holy place before Moses. If you trust in Jesus Christ alone as your one living hope of salvation on this earth—the only chance at forgiveness, the way, the truth, and the life, the pearl of great price for which you would give your all—then this is true of *you*.

So why don't we look holy? Why don't our faces shine like Moses? Or, perhaps more importantly, why don't we resemble the character of Christ that is so wildly different from the world that it would instantly set us apart from a crowd? First of all, we need to realize that when Jesus cried, "it is finished," on the cross, He meant it, and by His victorious life, death, and resurrection He purchased for us a perfect record before a just God and a new life in the spirit. In the spirit, we are one with Christ. But we are not only spiritual creatures, and our bodies are yet fallen. With that in mind, sanctification is the process, and humility is the key. To be sanctified is to be "set apart as holy," and sanctification in the New Testament speaks of the process by which we are made more and more like the Living God until the day on which we are fully united with Him in Spirit without fallen bodies to keep us down. But humility gets us there.

Humility Attracts Holiness

We have already established that God is far, far greater than any of us. But listen to this amazing verse sharing God's own words about His greatness and how He wants to relate to mankind: *"'Heaven is my throne, and the earth is my footstool; what is the house that you would build for me, and what is the place of my rest? All these things my hand has made, and so all these things came to be,' declares the Lord. 'But this is the one to whom I will look: he who is humble and contrite in spirit and trembles at my word'"* (Isaiah 66:1-2, ESV). God makes it clear that no man can really do anything for Him that He can't do for Himself. He doesn't *need* us. But then He says, "*this* is the kind of person I am looking for—" What kind of person? A humble one, one who trembles when God speaks, because they understand how great God is and how the tremendous power of His words can create and transform reality itself. God *respects* humility. He values it highly, so much that He is saying that quality alone will make him pay attention to you. And *that* is a truth worthy of *our* utmost attention, because I don't know about you, but I want God's eyes on me and His ears open to my cries.

Humility in the Bible speaks of a position of the heart. Humble hearts are "lowly," meaning they don't think too highly of themselves, as Paul admonished the Roman church: "*I say, through the grace given to me, to everyone who is among you, not to think of himself more highly than he ought to think, but to think soberly*" (Romans 12:3). Paul wants his audience to realize that they, honestly, are not very impressive—not before the God of the universe. That's sobering, but it's true. Humility is realism. It looks at the constant striving of humanity's sin nature for greater position and replies, "I have to accept that my place is down here, *not* up there."

Humble hearts resemble Jesus, who thought of Himself as

"gentle and **lowly** in heart" (Matthew 11:29). The humble heart does not lift itself up, but instead trusts God's Word in 1 Peter 5:6: *"...humble yourselves under the mighty hand of God, that He may exalt you in due time."* Humble people know their place in the world—in God's economy—and because they know their place, God promises to raise them up higher. It's like the story Jesus once told the religious authorities who enjoyed high positions: *"When you are invited by anyone to a wedding feast, do not sit down in the best place...But when you are invited, go and sit down in the lowest place, so that when he who invited you comes he may say to you, 'Friend, go up higher'"* (Luke 14:8,10).

This quality is what Jesus spoke of to the crowds in His sermon on the mount, *"Blessed are the poor in spirit, for theirs is the kingdom of heaven...Blessed are the meek, for they shall inherit the earth"* (Matthew 5:3,5). Jesus was promising the world to those who understood that they had nothing to offer on their own and who accepted their low place. The meek who choose not to reach for the things of this world will inherit the whole world. The Bible makes this message abundantly clear to us, and it makes the alternative clear as well.

What is the opposite of humility? Pride. What is Satan notorious for? Pride. He tried to get to a higher place, a greater status, the one he felt liked he *deserved*. It got him kicked out of heaven. and the end of his story is a lake of fire. What was Adam's problem that made him eat the forbidden fruit, causing physical death and cursing the earth? You guessed it. Pride. Adam and Eve wanted a higher place, to be like God. It's pride that led to every painful moment anyone has ever experienced or will ever experience in all of human history. Pride broke the world. And do you know what God hates? Read Proverbs 6:16-19, and you'll find that pride ranks number one on the list. But humility, on the other hand, gets you God's ear. Humility attracts holiness.

When God says, "*this* is the one to whom I will look, he who is *humble* and contrite in spirit..." He is opening the door to all of us. He is saying, "if you pursue humility, we can work together." Do you want God to do mighty things through your life? Do you hope to live a life of world-shaking purpose? Do you pray things like, "God, use me," but feel as though He hasn't completely answered you? Draw near to God, and He will draw near to you. Humble yourself, and God won't be able to resist drawing near to you.

When you lay your false self-importance down before the throne of the Almighty and say in your heart, "I know who you are, you deserve my devotion, and I have no right to even bow at your feet, but here I am—do what you will," it makes a pathway from God to you. He sees the empty well that you are and longs to fill it with Himself, because He is the Fountain of Living Water. Your lack calls upon His abundance. Your need moves Him to meet the need. And even as I say that, humility calls upon me to also say that men *do not* move God. Yet, God has revealed Himself in His Word, and He makes it clear that He *chooses* to move on behalf of those who humble themselves.

In fact, there is a passage of Scripture that much of the American church today is relying on for hope as the U.S. seems to be walking away from the Christian faith, and it's all about humility. *"If My people who are called by My name will humble themselves, and pray and seek My face, and turn from their wicked ways, then I will hear from heaven, and will forgive their sin and heal their land"* (2 Chronicles 7:14). Essentially, this was a call to revival for God's people before it was necessary, when Solomon and the people of Israel were committing their nation to serving the Lord. God knew that the people, however earnest at the time, would eventually walk away from Him and His ways. So He made them a promise while their hearts were receptive, letting them know that if they turned away, they could always turn back. He vowed to open the door of fellowship and grant them His blessing once again, if only they would humble themselves before Him by repenting, praying, and seeking His face.

Church people today want the land to be healed. They want things to get better. And God is able to do the impossible, though that doesn't always look the way we imagine it should. He is even willing to bring systemic change and restoration among His people, as demonstrated by His character in making the 2 Chronicles 7:14 promise to Israel, and we can trust God never changes. But He has standards, and humility is the way. We may accept this on first glance and thank God for His mercy, as we should. However, the next step we make requires great care. What we do next will determine whether we face the fire of God's judgment or feel the uplifting winds of His grace and favor. We must look within.

"The heart is deceitful above all things and desperately wicked. Who can understand it?" (Jeremiah 17:9). These words are the reason that we can't trust our commitment to humility. No matter how humble we think we are, we can't trust how we feel or how we see ourselves, because our hearts will trick us, the world will back us up, and Satan will drive the nail in the coffin with a smile and a wave. We have to make the decision to heed the Word of God in James 1:22-25: *"But be doers of the word, and not hearers only, deceiving yourselves. For if anyone is a hearer of the word and not a doer, he is like a man observing his natural face in a mirror; for he observes himself, goes away, and immediately forgets what kind of man he was. But he who looks into the perfect law of liberty and continues in it, and is not a forgetful hearer but a doer of the work, this one will be blessed in what he does."*

Letting the Word of God rend the darkness of our lives so the light of God can flood our souls is the only way to find humility. Humility grows as the Word exposes our sinfulness and highlights God's perfection. As holiness is revealed to our fallen minds and we stand in awe, we, like Isaiah, fall down before God in repentance from whatever lofty perch we may have grasped for ourselves, and we say with the prophet, "woe is me, for I am undone." That is the place at the foot of the cross where salvation is found, where a lost and desperate soul first trusts in Christ, and that is the same place where every Christian must live if they are to dwell close to God in humility. The truth is, because of the work of Christ that makes men righteous, God does not really care all that much how sinful you are, but He cares how humble you are.

Get Real with Yourself

Now, let's take that honest look in the mirror we talked about. Are you humble? Do you read the Word of God as regularly as you eat? Jesus said, *"Man shall not live by bread alone but by every word that proceeds from the mouth of God"* (Matthew 4:4). If this is true, is it not prideful to live as though we didn't need the Word as much as Jesus needed it, to eat and eat and leave our Bibles gathering dust?

Are you humble? When you pray, do you get disappointed that God didn't do what you wanted Him to do, what you desperately hoped He would do, sometimes to the point that you stop talking to Him altogether for a while? Is it not presumptuous of you to believe that God should do your will when you ask, but you don't mind ignoring the majority of His commands? Shouldn't a creature worship and serve their Creator, no matter what the Creator chooses to do with them? Does not the Creator deserve respect for even sending out the Word that formed the creature?

Are you humble? How often do you demand your own way, as though you were the most important person in the room? How many times has your spouse or children had to suffer because your will was not done, even though your will at the time had nothing to do with obedience to God's commands in Scripture? How many people have drawn your unseen wrath as though they didn't deserve to live because they cut you off on the road or disrespected you and your position at work? Do the people in line at the supermarket think you are humble?

It doesn't take long to see the point. The human individual demands special treatment because of the natural pride lurking in every heart, and this creates a sure barrier between them and God, the King of Kings whose authority is absolute. You and I are guilty of pride, and our way of life must become one of *continual* repentance and humility. We must continually fight the good fight against our flesh by mentally (and often physically) *lowering* ourselves. If we know Jesus and have become new creations by His grace, then there is a part of us that actually *wants* humility and aims for it. However, as Jesus reminded His disciples, *"the spirit is willing, but the flesh is weak"* (Matthew 26:41). This is why we can never quit fighting. Every day, the most important thing for that day is whether you humble yourself before the Almighty God who made you. If you do, you will find His grace sufficient for your weakness in every area of life. If you don't, you will strive and sweat and scream at heaven for what you can't get for yourself by your own power, and you'll often be angry at God for it as though it were His fault. Which will you choose?

If you choose the path of humility, you choose the path to holiness. God can draw near to you, and the Consuming Fire of His presence will change your very nature to make you like His own. You will become holy, as He is holy. You won't see the fullness of the promise on this side of heaven, but you *will* see evidence. After all, you are the light of the world, a city on a hill, a lamp that gives light to all in the house. God's work through Jesus Christ is so powerful, so final, your sinfulness is no match for the sanctifying power of the resurrection, and it *will* yield in battle after battle until His victory in you becomes clear—not for your sake, but for His name's sake.

Prayer Response

"Father, your name is holy; you are beyond me. No one is like you, and if it were not for your Son, I could not be near you. There would be a barrier between us. Thank you for tearing the veil! I choose to draw near to you, so I trust your promise to draw near to me and purify me with your consuming fire until only the indestructible character of Christ in me remains. I'm so thankful Jesus has made a way for me to be righteous, to share in holiness when I could never have touched it in a million years. I acknowledge that humility is the path to holiness. I want to accept my place before you and honor your place above me. I want to take the lowest seat so you can one day tell me to come up higher. Please forgive me for my pride, for believing so often that I was the most important person in the world, for lying to myself about it and living as a hypocrite, pushing others away from you in some measure. Lord, reverse that, and make me holy."

Chapter 5

Jesus Makes the Journey

"If you ask anything in My name, I will do it."
— John 14:14

Your journey to being purified is impossible. Isn't that comforting? Perhaps not, but isn't there always a sense of relief when you realize you can't carry a burden anymore? We feel that relief because it means we can lay the burden down. One of the most encouraging truths of the Bible was revealed when Jesus showed up in Israel doing miracles and began preaching to the masses in the cities where His disciples lived. He said to the crowds, "Come to Me, all you who labor and are heavy laden, and I will give you rest" (Matthew 11:28). What an offer! Can you imagine someone telling you that no matter what you are dealing with, they can give you rest *right now*? Think of the stresses in your life, the worries about the future and family members and money, the constant feeling of not having enough time or making enough progress, and then picture laying it all down so you can rest. That's the idea.

This is what Jesus came to do. Jesus came to bring rest and restoration to weary souls. And what's the area of greatest tension and burden for the human soul? Obeying God's law. That might not be the first thing that came to your mind when I asked the question, but every person feels a deep need to be *good*, to be *more* than they are. We all want approval, progress, and a good record. And for those of us who consider ourselves Christians, we certainly feel a need to please God. All of that goes back to what God built into the character of man, a desire to reach the standards that He sets for us as heavenly Father and as King. This expresses itself in a thousand ways in every area of life—even if we live in rebellion against God—in the same way that every child wants their parent's approval and strives for it subconsciously even if they deliberately live in such a way as to lose it.

We *need* to obey God's law. But we can't. And anyone that tells you different is selling something or has a pride problem, and their downfall is coming soon. This is why Jesus so soundly rebuked the religious leaders of His day, saying, *"The scribes and the Pharisees sit in Moses' seat. Therefore whatever they tell you to observe, that observe and do, but do not do according to their works; for they say, and do not do. For they bind heavy burdens, hard to bear, and lay them on men's shoulders; but they themselves will not move them with one of their fingers. But all their works they do to be seen by men"* (Matthew 23:2-5). These men were not only calling people to obey the hundreds of law ordinances handed to Moses during the time of the Exodus, they were also laying extra burdens on people that they'd invented as they sat in their studies "interpreting." Yet Jesus is clear: they could not keep the law, and they did not even try very hard, really, when it came down to it. Such is the way with mankind and religion. This is why the shepherds of the early New Testament Church met to discuss the requirements of the law for all who would trust in Christ, and their challenge in Acts 15:10 was: *"Why are you putting God to the test by placing a yoke on the neck of the disciples that neither our fathers nor we have been able to bear? We believe that we will be saved through the grace of the Lord Jesus, just as they will."*

So let's return to the marriage covenant we have made with Jesus. God calls upon us to express our covenant commitment and devotion to Him through the love language of obedience: *"If you love me, keep my commandments"* (John 14:15). But then God's own Word makes it clear that this can't be done. And where does that leave us? Lost and confused? No. Thank God for His Son, Jesus Christ! *"What the law could not do in that it was weak through the flesh, God did by sending His own Son in the likeness of sinful flesh, on account of sin: He condemned sin in the flesh, that the righteous requirement of the law might be fulfilled in us who do not walk according to the flesh but according to the Spirit"* (Romans 8:3-4).

What the law *could not do* (produce obedience in human hearts) because of the weakness of the flesh, Jesus *did*! Jesus came not to abolish the law, but to fulfill it. He became a man to handle what no man can handle, the task of obedience. People were created to be the obedient children of the heavenly Father, and Jesus became that good son. He did whatever pleased the Father, *only* whatever pleased the Father. He did everything that a person is meant to do, and He did it without fail for thirty-three years. This is how He is able to hand us the free gift of salvation and count us as righteous. We get to be welcomed into God's family and inherit the world and the rest of the kingdom as beloved children because Jesus did what it took to earn it. Isn't that good news?

But it's key for us to recognize and fight to believe that Christ's work did more than handle our eternity. When we are baptized *into* Jesus, when we become one flesh with Him in covenant marriage, the righteous life He began living on earth and continues to live now as a resurrected son becomes *our* life, today. Our spirit, our inmost being, joins with the Spirit of Christ, and this Spirit continues to live His life on earth *through us*. This is why Jesus said to His disciples before He died, "It is to your advantage that I go away; for if I do not go away, the Helper will not come to you;

but if I depart, I will send Him to you," (John 16:7) and it is why Paul could say, *"to me, to live is Christ, and to die is gain"* (Philippians 1:21). Jesus no longer has to walk around on earth in person, because He walks around on earth in millions of persons. And this offers us hope for the journey to purification.

Jesus Does It For You

Truly, Jesus makes the journey. If God desires obedience, we need only ask Jesus, and as He said, He Himself will do it. If the Father calls on us to be purified, then He Himself will purify us, and the Spirit of the Son in us will walk that narrow road and endure the sufferings that surely come along the way. And who is good at overcoming sin? Who has endured overwhelming suffering? Who has already grasped the victory in hand and defeated every enemy, even death? Christ in you, the hope of glory.

It is critical that we grasp this truth firmly in both hands and never let it go. Without the hope of the Gospel, there is no victory for the Christian today, no hope of holy living, no closeness with God the Father, and no chance at becoming a pure bride with a warm reception at the end-of-the-age wedding feast. As it is sometimes said, the Gospel is not the ABCs of the Christian faith, but the A to Z, and this is simply because Jesus Himself *is* the Christian faith. All the fullness of God dwells in Him, and He is the bridge from man to God. All the promises of God find their fulfillment in Him, and all creation is reconciled to God through Him and restored by Him in the new kingdom where He reigns over it and is worshipped forever.

So, let's remember the Gospel. God became man and dwelt among us, the only Son of the Father, full of grace and truth. He fulfilled all righteousness, and He then *became* sin though He knew no sin so that *we* might *become* the righteousness of God in Him. He was crucified, and God's wrath against the countless wicked perversions of all mankind across all time was poured out on Him in the spirit realm. He was buried, but within three days He rose from death because death could not hold Him, and He walked the earth again in a resurrected body, to be seen by hundreds of witnesses. He then ascended to heaven to be seated at the right hand of the Father where He always lives to make intercession for us, and where He waits until the fullness of time when all His enemies will be put under His feet and He will marry His bride.

For you who believe in this most sacred of truths, this means all that you once were has effectively died, the life you now live is Christ's life in you, and the future awaiting you is one where you live forever because death can't hold you and you inherit all things as God's child. For the matter of becoming purified for the wedding day, this means that every effort you make to be made ready for that day must receive all power to succeed from the life of Christ in you, and every thought given to pursue that goal must be submitted to the truths of the Gospel. This race cannot be run well except by the One who has run the race. So our goal is dependence upon and unity with Him, the Son.

These truths are easy enough to consider in the mind, but to live them out is another matter entirely. When I wake up in the morning, I need to tell myself, "you have died, and your life is hidden with Christ in God. The life you now live, you live for the Son of God, who loved you and gave Himself for you." My flesh and my mind *need* to hear this, and they need to submit to my spirit which is able to speak these things because of the Holy Spirit who dwells within me. When I begin prioritizing my day, I need to remember that this is not my day, it is Christ's day, and whatever I do, I must do all to the glory of God the Father. When the despair inevitably comes because I realize I can't do things for God today if my heart doesn't even care, I need to call on God, who is greater than my heart, to renew a right spirit within me, the very Spirit that Scripture tells me already dwells within me by faith.

Everything in your mind and heart are subject to the truths of the Gospel, and everything wrong with you is righted by the truths of the Gospel. Jesus is, *truly*, the way, for *everything*. And when Jesus says, "ask anything in my name, and *I* will do it," I need to take Him at His Word and ask Him! I can ask Him to parent my children. I can ask Him to love my spouse. I can ask Him to remove my anger. I can ask Him to produce joy in me where there is none. I can ask Him to overcome depression. I can ask Him to change the world around me to accomplish His will for my life. And the world moves. The joy comes. The love peeks its head out of my inner darkness and touches another life in a way I never could have because it just wasn't there before. And it all grows. The life of Christ in us increases, as John the Baptist once said, "He must increase, but I must decrease."

Today, when you put down this book, you can go to Jesus at the throne of God where He always lives to make intercession for you, and you can say, "Jesus, I *can't* do the next thing. I just can't. Will you do it?" And He will not disappoint you. It takes faith, yes, but even that is a gift. If you don't have it, ask for it! *"You do not have because you do not ask,"* (James 4:2). Let your prayer be like that of the man mentioned in Mark 9:24 whose child had long been mute and overcome with seizures, *"Lord, I believe; help my unbelief!"* When you doubt the Word of God for your life or that of your loved ones, you can tell yourself the truths of the Gospel yet again, and you can ask Jesus to give you the gift of faith.

So, truly, truly, I say unto you, be purified, *"looking unto Jesus, the author and finisher of our faith, who for the joy that was set before Him endured the cross, despising the shame, and has sat down at the right hand of the throne of God"* (Hebrews 12:2).

Prayer Response

"Jesus, I want to believe I can do it. I want to pick myself up when I fall down and move forward with greater purpose and discipline. I want to overcome. But I acknowledge right now the journey ahead is one I can't make on my own. I can't live a pure, holy life. I can't be a *good* person, a good parent, a good friend, and a good spouse. But that's why you came! You've done this already, and you *won*. I believe you can live the Christian life for me. I take my spiritual journey and place it in your capable hands. Jesus, please make me holy and purify my soul for your name's sake. The incapable person I once was has died on the cross with you, and my life is hidden with you in God. Overcome sin for me, change my heart's desires to match your own, and move my feet in obedience."

Chapter 6

For Better or Worse

"The Spirit Himself bears witness with our spirit that we are children of God, and if children, then heirs—heirs of God and joint heirs with Christ, if indeed we suffer with Him, that we may also be glorified with Him." — Romans 8:16-17

IT'S NOT ALL ROSES, THIS NARROW ROAD. It may feel like a killjoy to start a chapter with such weighty words, but we all understand that life is full of difficulty, and walking the narrow road with Jesus often brings more difficulty, not less. It also doesn't get less difficult when we ignore the truth. If anything, trying to live as though suffering isn't coming is perhaps one of the most dangerous things a person can do and one of the greatest downfalls of Western Christianity. Much of the internal struggle that we experience daily is due to our persistent efforts to avoid suffering and the inevitable failure of those efforts. Instead, we ought to start the journey with the perspective that Jesus *told* us to have: *"Enter by the narrow gate; for wide is the gate and broad is the way that leads to destruction, and there are many who go in by it. Because narrow is the gate and difficult is the way which leads to life, and there are few who find it"* (Matthew 7:13-14).

Jesus came to give mankind abundant life, the life we were made for and for which our souls yearn, but the path to that life is frought with difficulty, as it well should be. In what great story is there an amazing reward at the end worth dying for but which requires nothing of the hero? On the contrary, the stories that inspire us all are the ones where the victor triumphs over the most terrible odds and perseveres through the most intense suffering to reach rewards beyond measure. The obstacles overcome give value to the reward at the end of the journey. Jesus promises us trouble in this world, but He offers hope: *"take heart, I have overcome the world"* (John 16:33, ESV). He is hope in the midst of the trouble, and He is the source of overcoming power necessary to endure suffering, because He has already endured it, and He *won*. As the once popular Newsboys song goes, "On the road marked with suffering, though there's pain in the offering, blessed be your name." We can bless the name of Jesus all along this difficult and narrow road because of how good He is *on* the road. But it's a hard road, nonetheless.

Suffering is Against Our Values

Yet we try to avoid suffering at nearly any cost. Why is that? Answers may differ somewhat, but one of the main reasons for anyone raised in a Western nation is undoubtedly the press of culture and the habits of mind and heart with which we are raised. For most of us, the siren calls of comfort and ease have raised their voices since birth through every advertisement, authority figure, and formative experience of our lives—not to mention through the relentless march of advancing technologies. From Facebook ads touting miracle weight-loss products that do away with the rigors of exercise to tv commercials for exotic vacation getaways, the messaging is constant and clear: take it easy and enjoy yourself—you deserve it. Role models of success only further cement the notion in our minds as we value and tend to envy the incredibly wealthy and their luxurious lifestyles. Their stories surround us in every form of media, and their voice is given weight as though they had achieved something great for which everyone ought to strive. Then parents and leaders in the educational system tell children that if they work hard and get good-paying jobs, they can get what they want and be happy. When they get old, they'll be able to have some ease and enjoy the fruits of their labor. How many people are just waiting for retirement? How many people live for the next vacation? And we push forward farther and farther with technology, why? To make life easier. We want to get to the places we want to go faster, safer, and with less attention, so we built better and more powerful machines to take us there. We want to live longer and be healthier, but we don't want to change our life habits, so we need stints and pacemakers and diabetes medicine and CAT scans. We want that new phone or that app that can do that thing that we normally have to work hard to do. We want it faster, we want it better, and we want it more tailored to our unique wants and needs. The entire marketing industry is built on the idea that every business should get people exactly what they want, and the people expect the businesses to do just that. What's Burger King's slogan? "Have it your way!" The whole fast-food industry subconsciously trains people to despise one of the most natural sources of suffering in life: waiting.

So, when I ask why we're so against suffering, to say we come by it naturally would be a gross overstatement. But culture isn't the root, it's just the fruit that every generation keeps eating. The root is that age-old enemy of the human race, selfishness, empowered by the deceitfulness of the heart. Ever since the first man, Adam, people have made it their life's work to do one thing: satisfy their own selfish desires. Selfishness caused the world's first murder, raised up the world's first dictator, and led to the world's first war. If it wasn't for the fact that people can have children through acts of profound selfishness, I don't think the human race would have even survived this long. The most pervasive urge in any human life is selfishness, and you and I wake up dealing with it (or letting it run our lives by default) every single day. Now, I don't think it's too terribly hard for most of us to admit selfishness is a bad influence on the world, but here's the rub: *"The heart is deceitful above all things and desperately wicked; who can know it?"* (Jeremiah 17:9). The problem with us personally is not just that we are living selfishly, but that—most of the time—we *don't know it*. Consider an example.

Let's say a friend asks me to help them move, and I'm really busy and have other commitments, but I know the friend has no one else and expects me to say yes, so I do. I sacrifice my time and work hard to help my friend, but the whole time I keep thinking about the other things I should be doing, the people that are going to be disappointed that I wasn't with them instead, and I begin to resent my friend subconsciously for asking me to do this unreasonable thing. I get annoyed at little directives he gives while moving, even though, realistically, the direction is necessary to get *his* house moved properly. He should just be glad I am there. I start taking breaks to make phone calls, and I tell the person on the other end how it's the friend's fault we aren't done yet because he packs so meticulously. I share how I'm annoyed that I have to be at this another hour or two, but I am going to do it because I am a good friend. After that, I start thinking that my friend had better thank me well, and I expect him to have pizza or some sort of lunch delivered. Then, at the end, when he does neither of these things because he is swamped with trying to get his family taken care of and new obstacles keep arising, I leave in a huff, not saying anything, but thinking daggers at the fellow.

With all of that in view, can I say that helping my friend move was a selfless act? Not a chance! But I might move along, vaguely repentant about a particular thought or two I had that was less than gracious, and overall chalk it up as one good deed done that day. I'd deliberately look at the good things I did and ignore the terrible moments, and I'd rationalize it all away as best I could to quickly forget about it. This is the deceitfulness of the heart. From the start, the real reason I helped the friend was because I didn't want to seem unhelpful, and I didn't want to lose the friend's approval or get a bad reputation. Everything that came after that, no matter how well-intentioned I tried to make it, was tainted by the selfish heart I started with. And that example barely scratches the surface of the deceitfulness of the heart, as you well know from life experience. So, as we consider our selfishness and our inability to see it's pervasiveness in our lives, it's easy to see how the quest for comfort and ease has become nearly universal in our culture today. And the question is, what's wrong with that?

Let's explore our key text: *"The Spirit Himself bears witness with our spirit that we are children of God, and if children, then heirs—heirs of God and joint heirs with Christ, if indeed we suffer with Him, that we may also be glorified with Him"* (Romans 8:16-17). God's promises here are brilliant and precious. His Spirit that comes to dwell in every person who puts their faith in Jesus Christ is going to make sure we know in our heart of hearts that we belong to Him. He's going to make sure we know we are His children, and He'll remind us that being His children means we inherit all His Son is entitled to, because we have been adopted into the Son and stand before God hidden in Him. That's so *exciting,* isn't it? God is so good! As Ephesians 2:7 shares, God does this so *"that in the ages to come He might show the exceeding riches of His grace in His kindness toward us in Christ Jesus"* (Ephesians 2:7). He rescues us and gives us all this through Christ so that He can then continue to pour out kindness on us for all of eternity! What a Father! Who wouldn't want to believe that?

But is that all the Scripture says? In many churches where leaders give uplifting messages week after week based on Scriptures that they pick and choose, the explanation might stop there so that the focus might remain on something positive, because, after all, people are going through a lot in this world, and they need to stay positive. Sure they do, but how can we ignore the Word of the Almighty God? How can we leave certain truths be and make much of others when the same God who never changes saw fit to inspire men to write them both and charged other men to proclaim the *whole* counsel of God? No, the Scriptures continue after the precious promises of Romans 8:16, and verse 17 ends with a condition—IF. *If* we suffer with Him, we may also be glorified with Him. *If* we suffer with Him and are glorified with Him, we will know that we are among those in whom the Spirit is testifying that we belong to Him.

How could God put a condition like that on His promises? Isn't salvation by grace through faith alone, and not of works, lest any man should boast? Doesn't He so love the world that He gave His only son so that whoever believes wouldn't perish but would have everlasting life? Absolutely yes! God loves us and saves us by grace, but His Word never lies, and it says we must suffer with Jesus to get all of these other things that the preachers promised us we could get by just having a little faith in the Gospel. Did they lie? No, but some of them may have left something out. It's easy to do, because the doctrine of comfortable living runs so deep and is so covered up with deceit that most of us don't notice when it filters our portrayals of the Gospel and our personal testimonies of God's grace. The answer is simple: we must trust Jesus alone for salvation, and that will *always* lead to suffering. Both are part of the journey that leads to the inheritance we have been promised. In many ways, our faith is a great bargain: suffering now for glory later. We don't like to accept this. Even as I wrote this, I had to suppress the urge to delete the last sentence and say it differently, softer and somehow less ironclad. But there is no escaping this truth, and in the end, it is not so terrible as it sounds. We are just weaker than we ought to be, and we have drunk far too much of the Kool-Aid.

Our brothers and sisters in Christ around the world—especially in impoverished countries where the Muslim faith or Hindu faith are the norm—often see things completely differently. Now, their flesh is no less naturally selfish than ours, but by force of hard living before and after salvation through the lack of material wealth and relative dearth of technological advancements, they are less accustomed to comfort and ease. And because of the militant nature of certain faith groups towards professing Christians, not many consider following Christ without counting the cost. Therefore, those who have chosen to put their faith in Jesus are those whose fleshly nature has been weakened by constant lack and who have made a serious commitment to Jesus which to them is worth potentially losing their families, livelihoods, or even their lives. That kind of faith has no trouble believing that following Christ will involve necessary suffering. They expect it, and they learn to welcome it and endure it, if the Spirit of God dwells in them.

Western Christians, on the other hand, don't usually weigh the cost as heavily when they consider Christ. We may acknowledge that life will get a little tougher because certain sins will have to take a backseat to church gatherings and better behavior, but all-in-all, we expect to have our cake and eat it too. We want Jesus, and we want the life we were planning on having without Jesus. We want God's help, but we want it on our terms and for our goals. We want to serve God sometimes, even, but we want it to be fairly easy, and when it's hard, we wonder if we really have to do it. Perhaps He meant for us to do something else more suited to us and our preferences? After all, if we trust in the Lord He said He'd give us the desires of our hearts. And I don't desire suffering. We would like to do more for God, but He is going to have to take care of our money troubles and our health struggles. I need healing before I can do much else. Why won't God heal me? I asked already, several times. I even asked others to pray. I'm frustrated, because He keeps letting me suffer so much. Does this sound familiar at all? Do you think, on the last day, that God is going to evaluate us differently than our brothers and sisters around the world who are struggling through constant suffering with a joy that is "inexpressible and filled with glory?" I don't.

Embracing Suffering & Overcoming Sin

So let's take God at His Word. We must suffer with Jesus in order to be glorified with Him. The sooner we accept this, the sooner we can move on with our lives instead of struggling so hard every day with the unfairness of God allowing suffering into our world. We can begin to rejoice that God has allowed us to suffer with Jesus in order to be glorified with Jesus, and we can look to the glory promised to us at His coming instead of the fleeting relief we get when our present suffering ends for a moment. Every married person agrees to stick with their spouse through thick and thin, for better or worse. Those who leave when the going gets tough clearly didn't mean the commitment they made, and most of the time the reason their marriages fail is because they had the wrong expectations. They didn't *expect* so much suffering, and that's what killed the marriage, because suffering was always coming—it's what they signed up for.

When you yoke yourself to another selfish human being and allow them into the intimate spaces of your life, you are going to face some serious suffering as they hurt you and you hurt them. It's basic human nature. In the same way, a person who resolves to yoke themselves to a suffering Messiah for life should expect a life of suffering. Yes, Jesus said, "it is finished," on the cross in reference to paying the price of death for sin and receiving the wrath of God upon Him in the spirit, but He didn't mean all suffering was finished. He told His disciples that they would suffer much persecution, saying, *"remember the word that I said to you, 'A servant is not greater than his master.' If they persecuted Me, they will also persecute you"* (John 15:20) and *"if anyone desires to come after Me, let him deny himself, and take up his cross, and follow Me"* (Matthew 16:24).

Walking with Jesus means taking up a cross, and crosses cause nothing but suffering. They were instruments of torture, invented by the Romans to cause the most pain for the longest amount of time without killing the victim, so as to make a spectacle of the victim's death in order to instill fear in the hearts of conquered peoples. So no one takes up a cross willingly without good reason. And we have one! We are offered glory with the Son of God forever with an inheritance that is imperishable, undefiled, and kept in heaven for us! So let's take up our crosses. But how do we do that? Crosses mean death, and God says to every believer, *"you died, and your life is hidden with Christ in God,"* (Colossians 3:3) and *"do you not know that as many of us as were baptized into Christ Jesus were baptized into His death?"* (Romans 6:3). So, in one sense, this is a done deal. By putting our faith in Christ, we have taken part in His death. But there is more.

In the same letter where Paul tells the Colossian church that they have died, He then urges them, *"Therefore **put to death** your members which are on the earth: fornication, uncleanness, passion, evil desire, and covetousness, which is idolatry. Because of these things the wrath of God is coming upon the sons of disobedience, in which you yourselves once walked when you lived in them"* (Colossians 3:5-7, emphasis mine). Though the selfish, sinful people we once were have died, and we have been born again as new creations in the spirit, this old flesh is still ticking and causing trouble, so it needs to be put to death. Only our new spirit can do this, by the power of the resurrected Christ living in us who has already defeated every temptation during His own journey in the flesh. We must choose to take every thought, attitude, and action our flesh suggests and put it to death, because it does not belong. But this is difficult. I don't know how much you've tried it, but I've tried it enough to know that there is nothing easy about the process. And the Apostle Paul would agree.

He shares his heart on the matter in Romans: *"I delight in the law of God according to the inward man. But I see another law in my members, warring against the law of my mind, and bringing me into captivity to the law of sin which is in my members. O wretched man that I am! Who will deliver me from this body of death? I thank God—through Jesus Christ our Lord!"* (Romans 7:22-25). He's really struggling, and he's clear that the battle isn't one that goes away. It's always present, and he has no confidence whatsoever in his ability to win by his own strength. No, he cries out to Jesus in desperation because there is no other hope for him to escape his desperate situation.

Now, in case it's not on your mind, this is the same Paul who endured unimaginable suffering for the sake of the Gospel as a devoted servant of Jesus Christ, as he shares in 2 Corinthians 11:25-29: *"Three times I was beaten with rods; once I was stoned; three times I was shipwrecked; a night and a day I have been in the deep; in journeys often, in perils of waters, in perils of robbers, in perils of my own countrymen, in perils of the Gentiles, in perils in the city, in perils in the wilderness, in perils in the sea, in perils among false brethren; in weariness and toil, in sleeplessness often, in hunger and thirst, in fastings often, in cold and nakedness— besides the other things, what comes upon me daily: my deep concern for all the churches."* Yet, *this man* struggles with the daily battle of putting to death the flesh so that the spirit may live.

Every day, the Apostle Paul had to wake up, acknowledge his deep, innate selfishness, take it before Jesus who was crucified for him, kill it on the cross once again, and then go serve God in weakness. And so do you, and so do I. And so do the brethren in Iran, India, and China. This is the way. This is *normal* Christianity. Perhaps the most important part, though, is not that it's normal or that it's expected, but that it's *the only way* to victory. We all know that Jesus is the way, right? The Apostle Peter writes: *"Christ also suffered for us, leaving us an example, that we should follow in His steps"* (1 Peter 2:21). Jesus Christ Himself walked the road of suffering, and He didn't just do it in our place, He did it so that we might follow after Him on that same road. He succeeded where we would have failed without Him, and He now calls upon us to follow and overcome by His own strength within us that enabled Him to finish the race. Peter helps us understand why later in the chapter: *"since Christ suffered for us in the flesh, arm yourselves also with the same mind, for he who has suffered in the flesh has ceased from sin, that he no longer should live the rest of his time in the flesh for the lusts of men, but for the will of God"* (1 Peter 4:1-2). Did you hear that? Whoever suffers in the flesh *ceases* from sin? I can't believe it!

If you're like me at all, you're probably thinking something along the lines of, "I've suffered a fair bit in my life, but I haven't yet seen a moment where I've ceased from sin." Right, because the struggle against sin is not fully finished until we are presented blameless at the coming of our Lord Jesus Christ. However, the Scripture remains before us, and we must discover its truth. Let's look at the second part, the stated purpose of "ceasing from sin," which is to live out our days in the flesh no longer for our selfish desires, but for the will of God. Jesus did this every day, with one of the most notable moments coming in the garden of Gethsemane just before His death, where He said, *"Father, if it is Your will, take this cup away from Me; nevertheless not My will, but Yours, be done"* (Luke 22:42). In that moment, Jesus chose to live His life not for the passions of the flesh but for the will of God, as the verses in 1 Peter say. In that moment, He ceased from sin. Why? Sin is disobedience to God's will, a missing of the mark that God has set for mankind or for the individual. Jesus submitted His personal will in the flesh to God the Father, and in so doing, was without sin while His will remained submitted to the Father's will. His flesh suffered dearly in that moment, because its only longing was to get out of the path of the Father's wrath and to do something *more comfortable* than being ridiculed, embarrassed, and tortured as a public spectacle in front of everyone he cared about. But Jesus submitted His flesh to suffering, and sin had no hold on Him.

    Now, Jesus did this every day without fail, but it was still clearly a struggle there in Gethsemane, even though He was the Son of God in the flesh. It will certainly be even more of a struggle for each of us, yet the reality remains that we can follow in the footsteps of Jesus and submit our fleshly will to the will of Almighty God, and in so doing, cease from sin for a time. That's a miracle in itself! Unlike Jesus, our flesh eventually seems to win some battles, just as it did for Paul the Apostle, but as Paul himself said, *"this one thing I do, forgetting those things which are behind and reaching forward to those things which are ahead, I press toward the goal for the prize of the upward call of God in Christ Jesus"* (Philippians 3:13-14). We can submit our flesh to the necessary and daily process of suffering knowing that we are growing in purity as we aim for the wedding supper of the Lamb. And we can do it in the power of the resurrected Son! As the Moravians of Bohemia once cried, "Our Lamb has conquered all. Let us follow Him!"

Prayer Response

"Jesus, I'll be honest, I want it easy. My whole life, I've only known how to avoid suffering, to look for the quickest way out of pain or difficulty and to gripe about it until it's over. But that's not what I want my testimony to be on the last day. I don't want to pretend I am greater than you, and you said we would suffer because you did, that servants aren't greater than their masters. I accept this now. You are going to honor those who were willing to suffer with you. I want to be glorified with you! I want to share in your great victory because I, too, overcame sin and Satan and endured great suffering to reach the reward. Jesus, you are my reward, and your disciples considered it an honor to suffer for the sake of your name. Please, renew my mind so I can see it that way; change my heart so I can say the same, and *mean it*."

Chapter 7

Tried and True

"...for a little while, if need be, you have been grieved by various trials, that the genuineness of your faith, being much more precious than gold that perishes, though it is tested by fire, may be found to result in praise, honor, and glory at the revelation of Jesus Christ." — 1 Peter 1:6-7

BUT WHAT ABOUT EVERYTHING ELSE? This may have been on your mind as you ended the last chapter, realizing we talked about the stark reality of suffering for anyone following Jesus and what the Scriptures say about suffering in the flesh in order to cease from sin, but we didn't talk about all the other ways we suffer in life: the cancer, the losses, the broken relationships, and the spiritual attacks. The Bible has much to say about these as well, and they, too, are part of living out our marriage commitment "for better or for worse." In fact, this kind of suffering is really the main thing Peter is dealing with in the above verses from his first letter.

These early saints were experiencing all sorts of difficulties as they tried to follow Jesus. Perhaps the worst was persecution from their own people, the Jews. One day, they were brothers and sisters, one people against the world, everyone united by their common identity as children of Israel. Then, in a moment, everything changed. Not all that long after the early Church was established in Jerusalem through thousands of conversions to Christianity, a crowd took up arms and stoned Stephen—one of the early Church deacons—as he proclaimed the Gospel to them. The offense of the Gospel cost him his life, as it would many others in the future. The book of Acts tells us, *"At that time a great persecution arose against the church which was at Jerusalem; and they were all scattered throughout the regions of Judea and Samaria, except the apostles...As for Saul, he made havoc of the church, entering every house, and dragging off men and women, committing them to prison. Therefore, those who were scattered went everywhere preaching the word"* (Acts 8:1,3-4). What happened to Stephen was connected to Saul, a religious authority figure who was so zealous for the Jewish standards of law he would do nearly anything to uphold them, and it sparked a terrible wave of persecution that broke up the church in Jerusalem. The book records the Jewish Christians then took up residence in other nearby regions: *"Now those who were scattered after the persecution that arose over Stephen traveled as far as Phoenicia, Cyprus, and Antioch, preaching the word to no one but the Jews only"* (Acts 11:19). These people became known as the dispersion, those who had been dispersed by persecution from the original Church in Jerusalem.

Peter then wrote *"to the pilgrims of the Dispersion in Pontus, Galatia, Cappadocia, Asia, and Bithynia,"* (1 Peter 1:1) as he penned the letter with our text about faith tested in trials. These people know what it's like to suffer. At the very least, they've been confronted with their friends or family members being imprisoned, and they've had to leave their homes and start again somewhere else in order to avoid being thrown in jail themselves, or worse. They've had to deal with everything that comes along with that: facing potential poverty, finding employment and a new place to live, parenting children who don't understand what's happening, weathering the marriage struggles that come from extreme circumstances, and experiencing hunger and the dangers of the road. It is these suffering souls that Peter seeks to encourage.

Perhaps you have experienced some of the same things: homelessness, sickness, financial struggles, unemployment, and even hatred for your faith. The important thing is not to wish it hadn't happened or spend the whole time praying it'll all be over while hating every minute of it until it ends. That attitude flies in the face of what Peter is saying here: your suffering matters. It has value. It *counts*. He acknowledges this has not been a joyful thing, that what they've gone through has been grievous as they feel a sense of loss and a fracturing of life. But he doesn't conclude with, "hopefully it'll be over soon." No! He basically says, "it's hard, but it's worth it." How so? It's worth it because at the end of all things, when Jesus comes back riding on a white horse for a marriage feast with everyone He's invited into His Kingdom, our faith is going to result in praise! People are going to rejoice in Jesus and acknowledge the value due Him for sustaining our faith through seasons of incredible difficulty. Our faith itself is a gift, remember? Ephesians 2:8-9 says, "*...by grace you have been saved through faith, and that not of yourselves;* **it is the gift of God**, *not of works, lest anyone should boast*" (Ephesians 2:8-9, NKJV, emphasis mine). If our faith is a gift, then when it survives a trial, who gets the praise? The Giver. And if it endures struggle after struggle and still never waivers, then we are all going to be overwhelmed by thankfulness to God who was able to grant such strong faith to such weak vessels as we. These truths should help us grasp just how valuable suffering is for the Christian life, but I guarantee we don't fully understand the depths of it even now. You see, the one great purpose for all existence is the glory of God, the display of His supreme value as source of all good. As the Westminster

Catechism puts it "The chief end of man is to glorify God and enjoy Him forever," so when people *praise* God for what He's done, it's more valuable than *anything*. Your trial-tested, proven faith—God's gift to you—will achieve the greatest purpose for which you've been made: to glorify God.

The word "trial" in this passage speaks of an ordeal that tests the integrity of something, such as fire tests a metal. The fire shows how much heat the metal can stand, and Peter says here that if the fire gets hot enough, even gold will "perish" or melt, however valuable it may be. And even though gold is quite valuable, he's saying it's nowhere near as valuable as our faith, a faith that, it is implied, will not perish in the fire *however hot it gets*. It's an invincible faith, and we know that because it endures everything thrown at it. We know its "tested genuineness." We can tell it's the genuine, God-crafted article because of its ability to continue trusting in Christ no matter how hard life gets. And that means when you suffer, it matters. If you endure it, you're pointing to the King of kings, saying, "Look at *my* King! Look at what He was able to do! He gave me faith that nothing can shake." Please, allow this truth to settle in. Let it wash over all you've ever gone through and yield each trial up to Jesus as a sacrifice of praise for what He's enabled your faith to endure. You never again have to face something painful with despair, just wishing it would go away and wondering why God allowed it to happen. You can know the reason, and you can persevere.

When Jesus came the first time, countless prophecies had already spoken about Him, some of which are included in Malachi: *"the Lord whom you seek will suddenly come to His temple...But who can endure the day of His coming? And who can stand when He appears? For He is like a refiner's fire and like launderers' soap. He will sit as a refiner and a purifier of silver; He will purify the sons of Levi, and purge them as gold and silver, that they may offer to the Lord an offering in righteousness"* (Malachi 3:1-3). This Jesus sounds like the Consuming Fire that Moses warned about in the book of Deuteronomy. The people at the time were told not even to touch the mountain where the fire of God's presence appeared, or it would kill them. Even so, Jesus comes as a refiner's fire testing the thoughts and intentions of the hearts of men, and before him, nothing and no one could stand unless He made it stand. So we must praise God Almighty for having the desire and power to enable us to stand before Him by faith in the Son! Jesus gives us a faith that can stand in His presence, and He deserves all the praise for it when we survive a life of trials and enter heaven at the end of our time.

What to Do With Trials

So what should we do when various trials come our way? James tells us, and he also writes to the persecuted dispersion in the book with his name: *"My brethren, count it all joy when you fall into various trials, knowing that the testing of your faith produces patience. But let patience have its perfect work, that you may be perfect and complete, lacking nothing"* (James 1:2-4). This takes the matter of suffering a step further and helps us understand yet more of the purpose and necessity of it all. Not only does the testing of our faith result in praise for Jesus when He comes, it also *produces* something now, while we are dealing with the suffering here on earth. What does it produce? This translation says "patience," which is fine, but in today's typical usage, the word "patience" can sometimes indicate simply waiting until something passes, whereas this term is more powerful and active than that. It could also be translated as "endurance" or "constancy," and carries with it the idea of persevering *cheerfully*. We can think of someone running a race and having the endurance to keep running until the end because they expect to win. They are actively pushing through the obstacles and doing so with an attitude of victory. This is the kind of quality that trials of faith produce in the children of God. Doesn't that sound like something you'd want? If our whole life is bent on fighting the good fight and finishing the race, and if we, like Paul, want to press on towards the prize while looking to Jesus—the Author and Finisher of our faith—then this quality of character is not just good, it's *critical* for living. I submit to you that anyone unwilling to place value on endurance in the Christian life is running the wrong race, and they need to repent. If we would rather be comfortable than be strengthened to finish our race for our Lord, then we need to test ourselves to see whether we are in the faith. That is not to say that it is no struggle to appropriately value trials. This is why James has to urge the brethren to "*count* it as joy," because the harsh reality is, there is nothing that *feels* joyful about trials while they are happening, but we can take them aside in our minds and hearts to count them as joy by looking to the glorious product.

The passage doesn't stop with gaining endurance, however. It moves on to say that we need to "let endurance have its perfect work, so that we may be complete, lacking in nothing." This is astounding when you think about it. James is saying our whole lives can become more complete if we allow our faith to weather the test of difficult events. So instead of feeling overwhelmed, empty, and in need of a better set of circumstances that we fear no one—not even the Lord—will give us, we can face difficulty with eagerness, knowing each new obstacle is a chance to be more fulfilled in life. Somehow, Jesus's promise that He came to give us abundant life is fulfilled as we persevere through trials and are made more complete in the process. Somehow, choosing to stand in faith when the world and circumstances beat down on you with all their fury is the very thing that makes you more like Jesus, who won the title of Savior of the world by enduring trial after trial for 33 years and the ultimate trial of God's wrath poured out against sin. So don't let the Enemy steal that from you, and don't let the world steal that from you. It would be all too easy to do. Your friends will try to make you feel better the way they try to make themselves feel better, by saying they hope it gets better, but there is no power in their words, and sometimes it doesn't get "better," if better means less stressful or painful. They may even try to distract you, if you haven't already distracted yourself, through entertainment or busyness or relationships. Either way, by ignoring the trial or putting false hope in things changing a little tomorrow and making life a little less uncomfortable, we throw away the chance at growing our endurance and being made more complete by the trials we are facing. Let's not do that. Let's allow patience to have its perfect work, so that we may become complete, lacking in nothing. You won't regret it. The reward at the end is too great.

Endurance Leads to Fruitfulness

"For this very reason, make every effort to supplement your faith with virtue, and virtue with knowledge, and knowledge with self-control, and self-control with steadfastness, and steadfastness with godliness, and godliness with brotherly affection, and brotherly affection with love. For if these qualities are yours and are increasing, they keep you from being ineffective or unfruitful in the knowledge of our Lord Jesus Christ" (2 Peter 1:5-8, ESV). These verses help us understand how Christians can grow, and endurance is a key part of a bigger process by which God perfects us and without which we will short-circuit all that God wants to do in our lives. The term here translated as

"steadfastness," is the exact same term translated in the beginning of James as "patience" or "endurance." So when God says to rejoice when various trials come upon us because they produce endurance, that's the same character trait that Peter is saying will lead to godliness and genuine love.

If you could be like God in character and have unconditional love for your fellow men as well, wouldn't you say you had pretty much arrived? Endurance is part of the path. This passage in Peter could speak of a character progression of sorts, though some qualities certainly grow at the same time. Consider the beginning of your faith journey, if you know Jesus in truth. What came first? Faith. You received the gift of faith to put your trust in Jesus for salvation and to expect good things from God above. What did you do next? If you're like me at all, you asked God to change the way you were living, adding "virtue" or "good qualities and behaviors" to your life, and you spent some significant time working on that (it's still not over, by the way). If you were healthy, you also began to learn a lot more about who God is as revealed in the Scriptures and how it is that you're meant to live as part of His Kingdom. We could never stop here, because goodness and knowledge don't mean anything if you fall into sin and stop growing. To remain free of sin and to continue pursuing what is good, we need self-control over the wicked desires in our hearts. Thankfully, the Holy Spirit promises this as a fruit of the Spirit. We need only ask for it in faith and step out in obedience as though it has been given.

Finally, we reach endurance. As we supplement our faith with good character, good actions, and right knowledge while maintaining a level of self-control, it takes endurance to go any further. We need to keep going when the trials come, to continue increasing in these qualities when everything in life comes against us to make us quit. What's more, only endurance allows us to press on towards the highest forms of Christian character: godliness, brotherly affection, and love. The longer we remain steadfast on this journey, we begin to weather trials and face daily realities in much the same way that Jesus, our example, did it. In this, we are becoming like God. We begin to gain "godliness" as our character shifts to reflect His nature more than our former sinful nature. And it doesn't stop there, focused on us. No, the godliness being wrought within us will inevitably lead us towards what God cares about and push us outwards towards His other children, our brethren in Christ. As our affection grows and steadfastness leads us to show that affection to others on a regular basis, we begin to see glimpses of the highest ideal in all creation: love, unconditional, sacrificial love. This is the kind of love Jesus was talking about when He said to His disciples, *"As the Father has loved me, I also have loved you...greater love has no one than this, than to lay down one's life for his friends"* (John 15:9, 13). We can get an idea of the unfathomable depths of this love by exploring 1 Corinthians 13, which says that love endures all things. It never fails.

Ultimately, this process Peter describes is what keeps us from being unfruitful in the knowledge of our Lord. It's what makes our life count for something at the end of the line. We are on a journey, and the end is Jesus, both His presence forever and His character within us as we have been changed along the way. And this makes our suffering valuable. Everything difficult we face in life has the chance of making us like our Lord Jesus, increasing our character so that we are fruitful for the King and able to look forward to His coming rather than shrinking away from it. Let us embrace the trials as they come, *counting* them as joy and enduring them with a view to the end of the race. You will be stronger tomorrow if you do. But you can't do it alone. Only the life of Christ in you can sustain you to the end.

And so it is that we reach the end of the matter. Trials don't just make you perfect, they make you dependent. You recognize that no matter how valuable trials may be for the strengthening of your faith, you feel like they are beating you up and tearing you apart, and you are not enough. You feel the lack, recognizing in the midst of the suffering that you just don't have enough for what's next. You've run out of ideas. You don't believe the ones you have will work anyway. You can't get motivated to try them because of your despair. You fear that something outside of your control would stop you if you managed to overcome the despair. And there, at the edge of hopelessness, is Jesus. *"Have you not known? Have you not heard? The everlasting God, the Lord, The Creator of the ends of the earth, neither faints nor is weary. His understanding is unsearchable. He gives power to the weak, and to those who have no might He increases strength. Even the youths shall faint and be weary, and the young men shall utterly fall, but those who wait on the Lord shall renew their strength; they shall mount up with wings like eagles, they shall run and not be weary, they shall walk and not faint"* (Isaiah 40:28-31). Your weakness is a chance to see His strength. *"And He said to me, 'My grace is sufficient for you, for My strength is made perfect in weakness.' Therefore most gladly I will rather boast in my infirmities, that the power of Christ may rest upon me"* (2 Corinthians 12:9).

Prayer Response

"Father, it's been a hard road. So much has happened. Pain, sickness, and death have not left me and my loved ones alone, even when I've prayed. My faith has struggled to believe the best about you in many of these moments. I repent even now of believing anything less about you than the full truth. You are what you said, and more. You said my faith is precious to you. I want to believe that. You have sustained it through so much! Please fix my eyes on the end of the road. When trials come, grant me endurance. When I am tested, make me prove true. Teach my soul to count trials as joy, knowing they will make me more like your Son—more able to finish the race. Strengthen my faith and character until they can stand firm on the last day. May these growing qualities keep me from being ineffective or unfruitful in the Body of Christ."

CHAPTER 8

A Covenant People

*"By one Spirit we were all baptized into one body—
whether Jews or Greeks, whether slaves or free—
and have all been made to drink of one Spirit. For
in fact the body is not one member but many."*
— 1 Corinthians 12:13

YOU ARE NOT ALONE. Those are the words that every wounded veteran longs to hear, and the VA's 24-7 Veteran's Crisis Hotline aims to make sure they know it before it's too late. For men and women who have been battered and bruised by the traumatic experiences of combat and have returned to civilian life, suicide is a very real threat. Perhaps the most insidious lie that the enemies of the cross use to torment these troubled souls is the idea that there is no one out there who understands. They must struggle for their lives alone. Naturally, this leads people deeper into despondency and despair until they want to take their lives rather than face life without help and fellowship. And it is not so different for the rest of us.

If you've lived very long, you've met the emptiness of loneliness. You've felt misunderstood, betrayed, hated, or forgotten, and you've wondered whether you'll make it through the experience. In that moment, what you wanted the most—whether you knew it at the time or not—was to be *with* someone who understood you. You wanted to feel known by a soul that could see and acknowledge your pain, weep with you for a while, and offer you a measure of strength to lift your weary eyes towards a hopeful future. For most of us, many of these times in our lives were met with unfeeling correction from those that we thought loved us, blind indifference, or nothing, because no one was there who knew what was going on inside of us. By God's grace, many of us have also experienced rare moments of genuine understanding, comfort, and blessing through genuine followers of Jesus Christ who noticed us in our need. However, the weight of our experiences invariably pushes us towards the sneaking suspicion that there's no one out there who really cares about us, and the enemy of our souls uses this to manipulate us into thinking we don't need others in our lives—at least not *too* close.

No One is an Island

But what does God say? To the born-again follower of Jesus Christ, He says, *"By one Spirit we were all baptized into one body...in fact the body is not one member but many"* (1 Corinthians 12:13). When you professed Christian faith, you committed to "become one flesh" with the Son of God, to completely renounce your personal identity apart from Him in order to assume a new, unified identity as part of His Body. You were baptized into His life, death, and resurrection, and baptism is about *identification.* You washed away the old and took on the new. Now, your body belongs to Him. Your mind belongs to Him. Your spirit belongs to Him. It's not about you. It's about Him, and He deserves your devotion, yes, but He deserves more. He deserves the devotion of every person who's ever lived by the breath He provides. He deserves a Bride that represents the best of humanity, the unique, gifted, many-membered Church from every tribe and tongue across the world, all singing out in unison on their wedding day, "Worthy is the Lamb who was slain! Worthy is the King who conquered the grave! Blessing and honor and glory and power belong to Him!" He deserves a tide of testimonies from countless lives transformed by His grace through the ages. And He will have it, because you are *not* alone. The Body is not one member, but many.

When you chose the narrow path, you joined a great cloud of witnesses from thousands of years of Church history who were adopted together into God's family and unified in the life of Christ, inextricably linked together as a Body is linked together: *"For as the body is one and has many members, but all the members of that one body, being many, are one body, so also is Christ "* (1 Corinthians 12:12). This means you are not allowed to think of yourself and your "personal" walk with Jesus in singular, unattached terms. This isn't just *your* life, it isn't just your decision, and it isn't just your sin that only affects you. That would be the equivalent of your hand making its own plans without regard to your brain, your ears, or your legs. Needless to say, the hand wouldn't get very far. And if your hand was somehow able to murder someone or steal something, your whole body would get thrown into jail, because even the law acknowledges the body is a unit.

This is why Paul continues on in his letter to the Corinthians to say, *"If the foot should say, 'Because I am not a hand, I am not of the body,' is it therefore not of the body? And if the ear should say, 'Because I am not an eye, I am not of the body,' is it therefore not of the body? If the whole body were an eye, where would be the hearing? If the whole were hearing, where would be the smelling? But now God has set the members, each one of them, in the body just as He pleased. And if they were all one member, where would the body be? But now indeed there are many members, yet one body. And the eye cannot say to the hand, 'I have no need of you'; nor again the head to the feet, 'I have no need of you'* (1 Corinthians 12:15-21). He's writing this to let people know that every member of the Body counts and is necessary, which should be obvious, but God knew that people would struggle with looking at themselves and thinking of themselves as separate or as unimportant in their function, and He made sure to provide us with truth beforehand to combat the lies that would inevitably spring up in our deceitful hearts. So when we hear the lie of our Western, individualized culture saying, "you're on your own; just keep looking out for number one," we can confidently respond, "I am not alone! I am just one part of the many-membered Body of Christ, and He reigns in victory over temptation, Satan, and the grave!"

This is so very important for us to grasp, because Jesus *can't* be represented rightly by an individual. You might say, "God can't be rightly represented by people at all, so what's your point?" and that would have some sense to it, but listen to this: *"And He [the Father] put all things under His [the Son's] feet, and gave Him [the Son] to be head over all things to the church, which is His body, the fullness of Him who fills all in all"* (Ephesians 1:22-23). Did you catch that? The Church is the fullness of Jesus, who fills all and is in all. I wouldn't believe it if I didn't have to, because of how little I have seen of the fullness of Christ in the people around me, but I trust the Word of God, and God is saying here that the Body of Christ is the fullness of Christ. Jesus lives within every member of His Body, and if you could look at us together in one glance the way God the Father can from heaven, you would see His Son. Imagine one of the resurrection eyewitnesses capturing a perfect picture of Jesus in His glorified body then taking it to a glassmaker to craft a beautiful, stained-glass mural. If you could assemble together the scattered children of God from around the world in one place, you would see that same image. As things stand, it's almost as if the mural was shattered into a million pieces, and those pieces have been dispersed to communities around the world, some falling into hidden places where there aren't many counterparts and others landing together and forming a sizeable section of the mural. Regardless, what any given person may see of Christ's image, it will be incomplete until the day He returns and calls all of His people together at the wedding supper. But *every single person* is a piece of the picture, even now, and we owe it to Jesus to present a more complete picture to the world.

The Invisible Made Visible

Consider the Apostle John's promise to the early church: *"No one has seen God at any time. If we love one another, God abides in us, and His love has been perfected in us"* (1 John 4:12). First, we hear what we already know: nobody has seen God. Right, that's clear enough. To Moses, God said, *"You cannot see My face; for no man shall see Me, and live"* (Exodus 33:20). But didn't Jesus manifest the Father in the flesh? Yes! *"No one has seen God at any time. The only begotten Son, who is in the bosom of the Father, He has revealed Him"* (John 1:18), because *"He is the image of the invisible God"*

(Colossians 1:15). Jesus changed this whole equation, because He displayed who God really is *in the flesh*, in a way that can be seen with the human eye. Then He left. He died, rose, and went to heaven! And where does that leave the world? How will they know the Father? Jesus is still here on earth, showing the world who the Father is and drawing them to Himself—in His *Body*, the Bride of Christ! Let's go back to 1 John 4:12 where the author acknowledges no one has seen God. He then makes a promise: "if we love one another, God's love is perfected (or made complete) in us." God is saying through John that when His people *really* love each other, the world sees the invisible God, because His love is on display in His Body here on earth. After all, *"no one ever hated his own flesh, but nourishes and cherishes it, just as the Lord does the church. For we are members of His body, of His flesh and of His bones"* (Ephesians 5:29-30). Every one of us takes care of our body; whether we hate the way we look or display any genuine care for our health or not, we still feed our bodies and give our bodies what we need to live and a whole lot of what we want, because we *value* them. It's time we accepted that we belong to the Body of Christ, and that there is a natural indebtedness to the other members of the Body that can only be fulfilled by sacrificial love. When we do, the world will know who Jesus is. They will see Him in us.

Not only is this right, it is necessary for the human soul to flourish. Everything you want in your heart of hearts is found through fellowship with God Himself in part through His Body on earth. As we said earlier in the chapter, at our worst moments, we need others. This is true, but it's also true that we need others in order to have our best moments, and not just any others—we need members of Jesus's body supplementing what we lack in order to fully display the truth of who we are together. When we feel a lack in ourselves, it's not something that needs to be fixed by the right pick-me-up talk or self-help book trying to bolster our self-esteem. The word "self" is far too prevalent in these sort of conversations to be of any real good. Ultimately, we need Jesus to complete us, and here on earth—on this side of the second coming—His people are *most* of what we get. Yes, we get the presence of His Spirit dwelling within us, as God promises to make His home in all who believe (John 14:23), and that is more than any of us could hope to deserve, but everything *tangible* we need to live out our God-ordained callings and feel fulfilled in life is found in the Body of Christ, the Church.

Love Takes Work

So let's stop pretending we don't need others and allow the Word of God to reshape our lives. It will be difficult, it will take time, and it will cost something. But it *is* worth it. And you made a promise. If you truly call yourself a Christian, a saint, or a child of God, then you made an unbreakable covenant with Jesus *and* everyone else who has or will ever believe. You agreed to become one with Jesus so that His righteousness might erase your sin through baptism into His death and resurrection, as Romans 6:3-5 shares, *"Do you not know that as many of us as were baptized into Christ Jesus were baptized into His death? Therefore we were buried with Him through baptism into death, that just as Christ was raised from the dead by the glory of the Father, even so we also should walk in newness of life. For **if we have been united together in the likeness of His death, certainly we also shall be in the likeness of His resurrection**"* (Romans 6:3-5, emphasis mine). You see, we have been *united together* in His death and resurrection. All of us went into the same water, spiritually, and we all come out as part of the same body, the Body of Christ.

"There is one body and one Spirit, just as you were called in one hope of your calling; one Lord, one faith, one baptism; one God and Father of all, who is above all, and through all, and in you all" (Ephesians 4:4-6). God couldn't be clearer about this reality. You and I are one in Christ. You and the Christian neighbor you don't like are one in Christ. There is no escaping it, so let's humble ourselves before the truth of God's Word about Jesus's finished work, and we will have His grace to overcome our selfishness. That's the hope of the Gospel! And what we are together is so much greater than what we are apart. *"But you are a chosen generation, a royal priesthood, a holy nation, His own special people, that you may proclaim the praises of Him who called you out of darkness into His marvelous light,"* (1 Peter 2:9). What a wonder! We are a special, holy, royal family of people

who together represent the Almighty God on earth! And all those promises we hope God will answer...those were promises made to His *people*, not just to you. Perhaps you might consider that next time you wonder why He hasn't answered as you hoped.

So where does that leave us? What can we do? Jesus made it simple for us: *"As I have loved you, you also love one another. By this all will know that you are My disciples, if you have love for one another"* (John 13:34-35). My natural reaction is to say, "Of course, I know I need to love others. I do in my own way, better than this guy over here..." But we are not natural people anymore, are we? The resurrection life of Christ in the believer is not a natural life but a supernatural one empowered by the Holy Spirit to live with the character of Christ. And Jesus said to love others in the same way He loved us. Think of what He did to show that love. He left heaven. He spent 33 years on earth in weakness, enduring splinters and sweat and stress, and He did it without once choosing Himself over another person. He sought and saved the lost. He set people free from addictions and demons and sickness. He confronted authority figures who were abusing their power at risk of his own reputation and his life. He was betrayed. He endured the unjust torture of being wrongly accused of a crime, punished, insulted, and ultimately killed. And He did it all for those He called His friends (John 15:13). That's what love is.

"Love suffers long and is kind; love does not envy; love does not parade itself, is not puffed up; does not behave rudely, does not seek its

own, is not provoked, thinks no evil; does not rejoice in iniquity, but rejoices in the truth; bears all things, believes all things, hopes all things, endures all things. Love never fails" (1 Corinthians 13:4-8). When your love looks like this, you know you are really representing Jesus. When was the last time you suffered long under the foolish behavior of a friend in Christ? How often does your pride demand that others give you your way because you know best? How easy is it to provoke you? Do you believe your brothers and sisters *first*, unless all else proves their fruit to be truly rotten? How much has your love for the church endured over the years—not survived, but *endured*, unwavering in strength as it grows with a growth that is from God? Once again, I doubt your answers would impress either of us, and that's why we need Jesus filling our mortal bodies with His life and love as we abide in His presence. The point is this: the love bar is higher than you know, and you can't reach it entirely, but the pursuit of that goal is what characterized the amazing Acts church that we hear so much about. Paul said it well, *"Not that I have already attained, or am already perfected; but I press on, that I may lay hold of that for which Christ Jesus has also laid hold of me"* (Philippians 3:12). Because Jesus laid hold of this level of love for us, we must strive to lay hold of that love for Him, for His Body. In so doing, He will be manifested in us—and the world will see.

Before we move on to what God can do with a willing heart of love for the Church, the pressing issue of church division must be addressed. Since the very beginning of the Church, the selfishness of its members has fought against the Church's goal: to represent Jesus on earth. Pastors have taught lies. Members have gossiped about their weaker brethren rather than strengthening them. Pharisaic religion has taken hold of those in authority and squashed the freedom and power of Holy-Spirit-led change. Well-respected brothers have been found engaged in adulterous relationships. These things tear at the Body in much the same way that people with suicidal tendencies sometimes cut themselves. It's wrong, but somehow we don't seem to be able to stop hurting ourselves. I say "we," because it's not *them*. It's never just those *other* people *over there* in *that* church who are causing trouble for the wider Church's reputation and making the lost world misunderstand Jesus. It's never just the people who hurt *you* either. They may have genuinely hurt you, and they may have really been in the wrong, but you've hurt others, even without knowing it, because you have sin dwelling in your flesh. Paul goes on about this at length in Romans chapter 7, and the reality is, sin is at work in all of us, and it hurts everyone else. **But Jesus paid for that.** He paid the price for every wrong ever done against you and every wrong you've ever committed against others, whether you did it by evil intent or carelessness. He took the wrath of God against those sins, and He did away with it. Now, there is no more wrath for the children of God by faith in Christ. There is only love from the Father, a love that disciplines as a Father disciplines His children—let us not forget—but only love. So not one of us has any right to hold anything against another child of God that God Himself won't hold against them.

The reality is, when we hold grudges against parts of the Body, we are holding grudges against Jesus. When we choose to ignore certain parts of the Body, we ignore Jesus. He said whatever we do to the least of His brethren we have done to Him. And everyone who calls on the name of the Lord Jesus in true faith in His finished work is a part of the Body. Denominational ties mean nothing. Yes, certain groups stand well for certain great truths of the faith, and those truths are immutable and must be upheld, but no denominational group holds any sway in the Kingdom of God or rises to any loftier position in the eyes of our Father and King. So we must move past all that, applying the blood of Christ to every person and every wound, expecting that the all-surpassing power of His victory can bring healing and give value to everyone and everything. And we must move forward. But towards what?

What Church Could Be

In the book of Acts, the amazing story of Jesus continues in His Body, the Church. As He said to His disciples, it was better for Him to leave the earth so that the Holy Spirit might come and fill His people. Together, they would be mighty. And what was that like? *"...they continued steadfastly in the apostles' doctrine and fellowship, in the breaking of bread, and in prayers. Then fear came upon every soul, and many wonders and signs were done through the apostles.*

Now all who believed were together, and had all things in common, and sold their possessions and goods, and divided them among all, as anyone had need" (Acts 2:42-47). When the first 3,000+ people came to faith in Christ, they were described with the words from this passage. It's almost hard to believe, isn't it? People sold their belongings to give the proceeds to others? They didn't keep gaining and gaining for themselves but give a little bit away to feel better? No, they had *all things in common*. Later in Acts, the author describes this phenomenon with the words, "*Now the multitude of those who believed were of one heart and one soul; neither did anyone say that any of the things he possessed was his own, but they had all things in common*" (Acts 4:32). They believed that they, being one Body, owned everything together. "Mine" was not a category. It was only "we" and "our," and it was *voluntary*, not forced. I once experienced a small taste of this way of living in Washington state, where a church small group got together, laid out *all* of their assets (bank accounts, vehicles, stock, etc.) on a whiteboard, and asked the question, "Is anybody in need?" Someone was deep in medical debt, and they all banded together to completely pay the bill. Needless to say, the person whose debt was paid was speechless with thanksgiving, and they tangibly experienced what it meant to know Jesus Christ had paid their debt of sin.

What's more, these people in Acts were *joyful*, and they *enjoyed* being together. They ate their food with glad and generous hearts, going from house to house to fellowship. They were *devoted* to fellowship. With devotion, we're talking commitment to the point that everything else in life has to reshape around the objective. We devote ourselves to God alone, typically, and that only half-heartedly. But this passage describes a *devotion* not just to God and the things of God like truth and prayer, but also to experiencing each other's presence and sharing meals together. This is a whole new level of commitment to other people. And we have to take this challenge practically, one step at a time, one person at a time, one meal at a time, and one prayer at a time. You could try to live like this tomorrow with other people (we've tried it), and you would be disappointed beyond belief time and again by the selfish actions of others—even if you mean well—as well as overwhelmed by the selfish intent of *your own* heart if you could ever hold still in God's presence long enough to get a glimpse of it. We're just not that great. But then, we are amazing, beautiful, and special creatures, all at the same time. We are the best and the worst of this world, and God is madly in love with us. So we owe it to Him to try to let Him fill us with that same love for each other. But didn't Jesus pay it all? Yes, but this also is in the Bible: *"owe no one anything **except** to love one another"* (Romans 13:8).

This puts us in quite a position. We are no longer allowed to say, "it's *my* faith, and I can worship Jesus wherever and however I like." We must instead take a step in one of two directions: we can continue to live solitary lives that serve our own interests, denying the Word of God in order to please ourselves and blaming it on circumstances outside of our control, or we can accept that God is true though every man were a liar, and we can bow to His Word about our covenant with Christ and His Body, choosing to submit our own selfish nature to the goal of genuine love for others. We can find our place in the Church, doing our part to animate the great and glorious Body of Jesus Christ on earth today, accepting that *"we are His workmanship, created in Christ Jesus for good works, which God prepared beforehand that we should walk in them"* (Ephesians 2:10). Our destiny has been laid out for us, and it is a communal one. We can reach for the stars together, but only together. As we weigh this reality, let's finish with the ultimatum of Christ ringing in our ears: *"He who is not with Me is against Me, and he who does not gather with Me scatters abroad"* (Matthew 12:30).

Prayer Response

"Jesus, you said I could join your kingdom family by faith. I accept that this means I can't live as though my faith was private anymore. I repent. You've adopted me into a family! I'm one member of a body! I'll never be truly alone again. I have you, and I have your people. And *you* have *me*. Teach my soul the responsibility of this joint covenant. Teach me to become my brother's keeper, to live as though we were united by blood, because we are. Your blood is our bond, Lord. Set me in my appointed place in your Body, and show me how to serve you in a way that helps your people fully display your character on the earth. Renew my mind so I believe I need the other members of your Body, and empower me to love them well, no matter how hard it is. It's just as hard for them to love me, as you know. Humble me, and help me to honor them in my heart as greater than myself."

Chapter 9

In or Out?

"He who is not with Me is against Me, and he who does not gather with Me scatters abroad."
— Matthew 12:30

AM I PART OF GOD'S FAMILY? That's the question that should come to mind as we read Jesus's words in the above passage. He is drawing a line in the sand. You are either with Him, on *His* side, or you are against Him, siding with Satan, the adversary. Notice this is not about whether Jesus is on *your* side. It's about Him, and so our allegiance to Him is all that matters in this great conflict between good and evil. And He lays out the terms in a way that makes the conclusion inescapable—if we're honest. We know if we are with Him by our work, our way of life. Do we gather along with Jesus? Are we, in some way, using our lives and all that God has stewarded to us in a way that leads other people to join the Son of God's cause? The "yes" or "no" here is all that matters. Don't get caught up in the details. Some gather much more than others, and Jesus explained that too (Matthew 13:8, 23), but what counts here is whether we gather with Jesus *at all*. If you could get past all the deceit in your heart, is there even a chance that your answer is "no?" If so, there is but one conclusion: you are living a life that goes against what Jesus stands for, and you are driving people away from Him.

Let's return then to the original question. Are *you* part of God's family? Now that you know Jesus's terms, consider what answer comes to mind as you face that question. Did you hesitate at all? Or is it a quick "Yes!" but then doubts begin to cloud your mind? Does God's Spirit immediately rise up in you to cast down those doubts with His Word? This is *critical*, because God has promised to give His Spirit to every true Christian as a guarantee (2 Corinthians 1:21-22), a down-payment for the salvation and the kingdom waiting for us at the end of the age by faith, and *"The Spirit Himself bears witness with our spirit that we are children of God"* (Romans 8:16). The Holy Spirit of God Almighty will rise up within the true believer to tell them at their core that they belong to His family. He made a promise, and He always keeps His Word, so if you do not experience this, it is time to test yourself to see whether you are in the faith. This is not to say that the enemy of your soul won't come against you at times to cause you to doubt what Jesus has accomplished for you, but you *can* be confident that God's Spirit will overcome any such attacks to make you certain of His finished work on your behalf—unless you don't really know Him.

The Elephant in the Room

Western Christians don't like to deal with this idea, and they'd rather assume that they, their spouse, their kids, their cousins, and the coworkers and friends they're afraid to witness to are all, somehow, "saved." Wishing something is true, however, does not make it so, and no matter how "near" someone seems to belief because of their family or upbringing, nothing matters but their obedience or disobedience to the call of Christ to forsake all and follow Him. Jesus was clear: "***Not everyone who says to Me, 'Lord, Lord,' shall enter the kingdom of heaven***, *but he who does the will of My Father in heaven. Many will say to Me in that day, 'Lord, Lord, have we not prophesied in Your name, cast out demons in Your name, and done many wonders in Your name?' And then I will declare to them, 'I never knew you; depart from Me, you who practice lawlessness!'"* (Matthew 7:21-23).

Notice in this passage that the people Jesus is rebuking at the end of the age are not those who lived however they wanted and didn't give a nod to the Gospel. No, these are people who talked the talk and walked some kind of walk, "religious" people whose lives probably looked fairly nice on the surface as they did "good" deeds in hopes of getting a place at the Lord's table on the big day. But He cuts through their charade with the words, "I never *knew* you." That's the same term used in Genesis describing the way that Adam *knew* his wife, Eve. It's a complete, intimate knowledge of another, a connection between people at their very core. This is the same way that Christ knows His Bride, the Church. And if you can in any way say you are a Christian, a member of the Bride of Christ, then you had better bet Jesus *knows* you—through coming to live within you, through experience, through mutual sharing, and through walking the road of life together. Even if you just confessed your sins to Him and turned from sinful living to a life of faith in Him today for the very first time, that's a deep sharing of the soul, and you're probably closer to Him than you've been to anyone else you've yet known. Regardless, there is a closeness brought on by the miracle of Christ's death and resurrection that reconciles us to God by faith. And that closeness comes by *invitation*. We invite Jesus as Lord to know us, command us, and dwell within us. But for those who try their hardest to reach God in heaven by living good, religious lives, there is no intimacy between them and Jesus. He has not known them by invitation, and He will not know them apart from it. His love must be freely received.

There is another place in the Bible where Jesus is just as direct in challenging our commitment to Him, and it's at the end. Revelation 3:15-21 reads: *"I know your works, that you are neither cold nor hot. I could wish you were cold or hot. So then, because you are lukewarm, and neither cold nor hot, I will vomit you out of My mouth. Because you say, 'I am rich, have become wealthy, and have need of nothing'—and do not know that you are wretched, miserable, poor, blind, and naked—I counsel you to buy from Me gold refined in the fire, that you may be rich; and white garments, that you may be clothed, that the shame of your nakedness may not be revealed; and anoint your eyes with eye salve, that you may see. As many as I love, I rebuke and chasten. Therefore be zealous and repent. Behold, I stand at the door and knock. If anyone hears My voice and opens the door, I will come in to him and dine with him, and he with Me. To him who overcomes I will grant to sit with Me on My throne, as I also overcame and sat down with My Father on His throne."* Jesus here is speaking to the Church, so we know that He intends some of this to address believers. However, Jesus also said in Matthew 13:24-30 that there were tares among the wheat, which were unbelievers within the Church who would not be separated out until the end of the age. Therefore, whether we think we already belong to the family or not, His words challenge both our commitment level and our standing before God.

What's going on with these people that made Jesus say such seemingly harsh things? They're lukewarm. What does that even mean for a person? He helps us out with some details. For one, they have a lot of wealth, which may not be evil on its own, but there is no escaping the Scriptural fact that the *love* of wealth is *a* root of *all kinds* of evils (1 Timothy 6:10). And these folks really love their wealth; just listen to them: "I'm so wealthy I don't need anything at all! Why should I get on my knees and cry out to God? I can take care of myself." Jesus said these people appeared to need nothing, but in reality they were poor, blind, and naked in the spirit. Their true selves had little if anything of lasting value to offer. What they needed was to admit their desperate state and go to Jesus for help. This is always how people come to the cross, broken and hungry for help, believing at last that it will only come from God Almighty. Somehow, these believers had either forgotten that, or they were not believers at all. So we must ask ourselves, do we live in a state of dependence, desperately clinging to Jesus to meet the deep needs of our souls? Or do we mostly live as though we could take Him or leave Him? If Christ's resurrection could be proved false tomorrow, would anything drastically change in your daily life?

Jesus also asked these lukewarm people to open the door to Him so they could eat and fellowship together. This is a mark of intimacy, of *knowing*. If you remember, Jesus said in Matthew 7:21-23 that He "never knew" those people who had done all those seemingly great things. These lukewarm people, similarly, are not allowing Jesus into their intimate space to be known by Him. So, again, you and I have to face the question: am I intimate with

Jesus? Can I easily say He knows me, and I know Him? If this is not easy to answer, then God has another Word for us: *"Examine yourselves as to whether you are in the faith. Test yourselves"* (2 Corinthians 13:5). Do you hear that? We are called to look closely at ourselves in the mirror and test ourselves to see whether we really know Jesus. God isn't doing His best to remove our doubts by reminding us of a time we prayed a prayer of repentance and faith in the Gospel, which means, by the way, that we shouldn't do that either—for ourselves or anyone else. No, He is calling us to challenge ourselves, trusting that genuine faith will survive the challenge.

How do we do that? It starts with really *facing* God's Word. Hebrews 4:12 tells us *"The word of God is living and powerful, and sharper than any two-edged sword, piercing even to the division of soul and spirit, and of joints and marrow, and is a discerner of the thoughts and intents of the heart."* God's Word gets past all the deceit of our hearts to the core of who we are, and it changes us. It also helps us to see ourselves clearly, as James 1:22-25 shows us: *"But be doers of the word, and not hearers only, deceiving yourselves. For if anyone is a hearer of the word and not a doer, he is like a man observing his natural face in a mirror; for he observes himself, goes away, and immediately forgets what kind of man he was. But he who looks into the perfect law of liberty and continues in it, and is not a forgetful hearer but a doer of the work, this one will be blessed in what he does."*

God's Word acts as a mirror to overcome our personal

blindness, but it only has an effect on us *if* we do what it prompts us to do. As we submit to the process of letting the Word pierce us and prompt us to action, and we actually do what it says, we are being *tested*. That term used in the above verse, "test yourselves," is a term also used for testing silver in a fire so that all impurities are removed and only pure, valuable metal remains. When we allow ourselves to be tested by the Word of God, proving our faith by action as James says later in 2:18, *"...someone will say, 'You have faith, and I have works.' Show me your faith without your works, and **I will show you my faith by my works**,"* then that genuine faith planted in our souls by Jesus Christ *will prove true*. Nothing can dislodge it. And this is something that is evident in the life of a true believing Christian. For the one who does not believe, they will either not submit to the testing, or when tested, their faith will fail. The works of true faith are obvious, and we can know whether we are in the faith.

How to Know That You Know

If you really want to understand God's heart on this subject, He's got a single book in the Bible that can handle the whole matter for anyone: 1 John. The author makes this obvious at the very end of the book, summing it up with these words: *"These things I have written to you who believe in the name of the Son of God,* ***that you may know that you have eternal life****, and that you may continue to believe in the name of the Son of God"* (1 John 5:13). I believe if you will slowly and thoroughly read 1 John with a heart ready to have God reveal the state of your soul, you will finish it knowing the truth regarding your salvation and place in His family. Every one of the book's five chapters deals with this topic in some way. Right out of the gate, the author says in 1 John 1:5-7: *"This is the message which we have heard from Him and declare to you, that God is light and in Him is no darkness at all. If we say that we have fellowship with Him, and walk in darkness, we lie and do not practice the truth. But if we walk in the light as He is in the light, we have fellowship with one another, and the blood of Jesus Christ His Son cleanses us from all sin."* There's the first sign of your situation. If you walk in darkness, you don't have fellowship with Jesus. Remember the Word is a lamp to our paths, so if we walk in the light of the Word, allowing it to reveal our true state on a regular basis, we can have fellowship with others who see themselves and us more clearly, and Jesus's blood cleanses us from sin. Walking in the light doesn't mean walking sinlessly; in fact, the very next verse says, *"If we say that we have no sin, we deceive ourselves, and the truth is not in us"* (1 John 1:8). But it *does* mean that we confess our sin openly and allow God to change us.

If the question "do you walk in darkness or in light?" stumps you somewhat, you should have an easier time understanding the second chapter, where John says, *"Now **by this we <u>know</u> that we know Him**, if we keep His commandments. He who says, 'I know Him,' and does not keep His commandments, is a liar, and the truth is not in* *him. But whoever keeps His word, truly the love of God is perfected in him. By this we know that we are in Him. He who says he abides in Him ought himself also to walk just as He walked*" (1 John 2:3-6). You know how people in romance movies like to talk about "how you know that you know that they're the one?" Well, John is saying here that you can "know that you know" you're in covenant relationship with Jesus by whether you keep His commands. We all make many sinful choices even if we follow Jesus—some of them on purpose. The Apostle Paul was the one who said in Romans that he kept doing the evil things he did not want to do. God doesn't hide the imperfect reality of the Christian life. But this passage is about the heart. Do you see Jesus as your Lord, to the point that you *live* to keep His commands? Do you regularly wake up and say, "Lord, what do you want for my life today?" and strive to walk that out through meditating on the Scriptures and attempting to obey them? Or do God's commands function more like *suggestions* to you practically?

We can understand this dynamic better if we jump ahead in the book to 1 John 3:7-8, "*Little children, let no one deceive you. He who practices righteousness is righteous, just as He is righteous. He who sins is of the devil, for the devil has sinned from the beginning.*" The key word to note here is "practice." The one who tries over and over again to live righteously—by faith in Jesus Christ's strength within us, not by religious works done in our own strength—is righteous, just as Christ is righteous. We are to walk in the same way in which Jesus walked, which was a path of constantly striving to live a righteous life obeying the commands of the Father. Jesus *always* did what pleased God, but we can *always* practice doing so, even though we will often fail. People practice things they want to eventually master, knowing they will never be perfect, but striving for the standard. This is what marks the person made righteous by the finished work of Christ. They will practice His way, whereas those who do not belong to God's family will practice the way of the world, the way of the Devil. People are either doing one or the other. The reality is, if you don't *practice* righteousness, then you're regularly aiming at sin, trying to live a life *for* yourself by your own power under your authority, and *that* is why Jesus said whoever does not gather with Him scatters.

If these truths are leading you to the conclusion that you are not practicing righteousness and, thereby, are causing you to question your salvation, you may find your soul *screaming* for justification. Many of us will make excuse after excuse for not meeting the Scriptural standard, and we will hold ourselves up against others we know have failed so that we can feel good enough. If this is going on inside your heart right now, this is what *pride* looks like, and pride makes it *very hard* for people to be saved. The one thing that keeps a person on the road to hell is what put Satan on that road: pride. You are going to have to swallow that and ask God to humble you if you want any hope of eternal life. The same goes for the one who knows Jesus but struggles with pride. Eternal life may be secured, but pride is your sure downfall, and only humility will overcome.

All pride laid aside, let's return to the main message of 1 John. We who truly believe will practice keeping God's commands, and in so doing, we will love God. *"He who has My commandments and keeps them, it is he who loves Me. And he who loves Me will be loved by My Father, and I will love him and manifest Myself to him"* (John 14:21). If we *do* love God, 1 John helps us understand that at least two other things will most certainly be true of us: we will love our brethren, and we will not love the world. The author says in 1 John 4:7-8, *"Beloved, let us love one another, for love is of God; and everyone who loves is born of God and knows God. He who does not love does not know God, for God is love."* Did that register? Whoever does not love does not know God. In case the character of true love escapes you, God says, *"By this we know love, because He laid down His life for us. And we also ought to lay down our lives for the brethren. But whoever has this world's goods, and sees his brother in need, and shuts up his heart from him, how does the love of God abide in him?"* (1 John 3:16-17). This is not some self-serving emotion-based love that remains only so long as the lover is pleased with the object of their love. No! It's a love that comes from God's own heart, unconditional and ready to lay itself down in selfless service to others. If you belong to the Body of Christ, then you are one with millions of other people, and you owe them a debt of love. What's more, your fulfillment of that obligation to your brethren is one of the primary ways you can be certain you are part of that Body.

We also know that if we love God, we will not love the world. The admonition in 1 John 2:15-16 is blood-chilling: *"Do not love the world or the things in the world.* **If anyone loves the world, the love of the Father is not in him.** *For all that is in the world—the lust of the flesh, the lust of the eyes, and the pride of life—is not of the Father but is of the world."* This may have you thinking, "You're telling me that is one of the markers for whether I'm a Christian? I can't believe it! What about the gourmet food I crave, the pricey cars I long to drive, the bigger house I wish I had, and the impressive standard I'm reaching for as I raise my kids to do and be 'the best?' Are you saying I can't want those things?" The reality is, God is saying you can't love those things. You can't love the material things you can see, because we are not of this world, and God is your portion—if you belong to Him. Perhaps you do see a love for these things in your life. If so, you'd better heed the Word of God and change your mind towards Him now, before it's too late. *"No one can serve two masters; for either he will hate the one and love the other, or else he will be loyal to the one and despise the other. You cannot serve God and mammon [material things]"* (Matthew 6:24). When Jesus comes back, you don't want to be found naked because all the riches you stored up for yourself burned up in the fires of judgment. You'll want to know you are on God's side, because you loved Him while you lived.

A New Birth and a New Spirit

This will only be true of us if we have a second birth. As John declared the words of Jesus to Nicodemus in his Gospel, "you must be born again," so he continues the conversation here in 1 John 3:9, *"Whoever has been born of God does not sin, for His seed remains in him; and he cannot sin, because he has been born of God."* This is in the context of *practicing* righteousness rather than sin, so when the author says whoever has been born of God does not sin, in context he means whoever has been born again will not practice sin but will, rather, practice a lifestyle of righteousness. And this new birth will not only bring with it obedience, but a new spirit. *"By this we know that we abide in Him, and He in us, because He has given us of His Spirit"* (1 John 4:13). The Spirit of God comes to dwell in the true believer, and that Spirit has a very specific message: it confesses that Jesus is the Son of God, as the following verse shares, *"Whoever confesses that Jesus is the Son of God, God abides in him, and he in God"* (1 John 4:15). We can know that we "abide" or "dwell" in God by whether we confess Jesus as God's son with genuine hearts inspired by the Spirit living in us.

In the end, all we really need to know is this: *"He who has the Son has life; he who does not have the Son of God does not have life"* (1 John 5:12). As Jesus said to Nicodemus, *"God did not send His Son into the world to condemn the world, but that the world through Him might be saved. He who believes in Him is not condemned; but he who does not believe is condemned already, because he has not believed in the name of the only begotten Son of God"* (John 3:17-18). You need Jesus, and if you have Him, you have everlasting hope of eternal life that will never fade. If you do not have Him, you will one day wish you had chosen to be with him now.

At the end of time, there will be two suppers. Both are described in Revelation 19. The first is the subject of this book, the wedding supper of the Lamb, and all who trust in Jesus Christ's finished work now will be there as the bride to unite with the Groom who held her hand through thick and thin in life and who will now hold it in holy matrimony for all of eternity. Revelation 19:6-9 describes this wonderful event: *"And I heard, as it were, the voice of a great multitude, as the sound of many waters and as the sound of mighty thunderings, saying, 'Alleluia! For the Lord God Omnipotent reigns! Let us be glad and rejoice and give Him glory, for the marriage of the Lamb has come, and His wife has made herself ready.' And to her it was granted to be arrayed in fine linen, clean and bright, for the fine linen is the righteous acts of the saints. Then he said to me, 'Write: 'Blessed are those who are called to the marriage supper of the Lamb!'"*

Then, there is the other supper described in the same chapter. That supper also starts with Jesus's appearance, but rather than arriving as the Faithful Bridegroom, He arrives as Judge and General, mounted on a white horse leading the armies of God against those who have rebelled against His authority on earth.

The passage reads, "Now I saw heaven opened, and behold, a white horse. And He who sat on him was called Faithful and True, and in righteousness He judges and makes war...Then I saw an angel standing in the sun; and he cried with a loud voice, saying to all the birds that fly in the midst of heaven, 'Come and gather together for the supper of the great God, that you may eat the flesh of kings, the flesh of captains, the flesh of mighty men, the flesh of horses and of those who sit on them, and the flesh of all people, free and slave, both small and great.' And I saw the beast, the kings of the earth, and their armies, gathered together to make war against Him who sat on the horse and against His army. Then the beast was captured, and with him the false prophet who worked signs in his presence, by which he deceived those who received the mark of the beast and those who worshiped his image. These two were cast alive into the lake of fire burning with brimstone. And the rest were killed with the sword which proceeded from the mouth of Him who sat on the horse. And all the birds were filled with their flesh" (Revelation 19:11, 17-21). This scene describes God's judgment against those who allowed themselves to be deceived into following their own way rather than submitting to the Lordship of Jesus Christ. The way they chose ends with them being eaten by vultures. I think I know which supper I'd like to attend, and only Jesus, precious Jesus, can secure the way for me—or for you.

Prayer Response

A prayer of examination:

"Father, help me examine myself; test whether I am in the faith. Have I loved the brethren, or is your love not in me? Do I confess that Jesus is your risen Son? Have I gathered with you at all? Or do I scatter those who might come to you because of the hypocrisy in my heart? You know me, Lord, better than I know myself. Lay bare my soul so that I might be certain of my eternal destiny. Reveal to me the truth about my relationship with you. You deserve servants that will gather in your harvest with you. Make me one!"

A prayer of repentance and faith:

"Father, I've been found out. I recognize the lack of wholeness in my life. I am not connected to you, the true source of life. I have lied to myself and others about being a Christian, believing I was somehow good enough by works. I turn away from the lies today! I surrender to you, Jesus. I choose to entrust my whole existence to you. I can't save myself, so please rescue me, Jesus! I believe you lived the perfect life in my place. I believe you died to take the judgment of God against my sin. I believe you rose from the dead to defeat death and give me eternal life!"

Chapter 10

The Best Man

"He who has the bride is the bridegroom; but the friend of the bridegroom, who stands and hears him, rejoices greatly because of the bridegroom's voice. Therefore this joy of mine is fulfilled."
— John 3:29

ARE YOU A SHEPHERD? If your answer is "yes" or "maybe," then this chapter is for you. If your answer is a confident "no," then you may wish to move on to the next chapter so as not to lose momentum, as much of the contents of Chapter 10 only applies to those who lead the church in a shepherding capacity. The character-building principles within this chapter, however, apply to all.

Be careful how you answer the above question; it comes with weight. Jesus, after all, is the Good Shepherd who leads His people from the front, going before them into danger, suffering for their sakes, guiding them to places where their every need is met, feeding them with knowledge and understanding. Those who call themselves shepherds must accept that their primary purpose is to bear the image of Jesus, the Good Shepherd. Every way in which their lifestyle and work deviates from the life and work of Christ is an affront to His name, and every way in which it conforms to His way will glorify His name as He is represented on earth through these members of His Body.

Keep in mind, everyone who wants or allows the term "pastor" to be a part of their title is assuming the position of shepherd since they are synonymous, and anyone who would be an elder or overseer—a person entrusted with authority in the family of God—is called to the work of a shepherd (1 Peter 5:1-2). And every shepherd must be able to teach (2 Tim. 2:24), because part of their calling is feeding the flock with knowledge and understanding as the Good Shepherd does. This means that God's admonition through James applies to every would-be shepherd: "*My brethren, let not many of you become teachers, knowing that we shall receive a stricter judgment. For we all stumble in many things. If anyone does not stumble in word, he is a perfect man, able also to bridle the whole body*" (James 3:1-2). It is a grave thing to assume the responsibility of guiding God's people into the truth—of stewarding the mysteries of God, as Paul put it. It is, however, one of the greatest privileges afforded a man, to commune with God and speak for Him to His people. We'd just better be certain it is our God-given role—or else.

Considering the parable of the bride given at the beginning of this book, John's words at the opening of this chapter highlight for us the heart a shepherd must have. When he describes the friend of the bridegroom, he is describing himself, tasked with proclaiming to God's people His Word for their time as a prophet and teacher. John was Jesus's friend, and we must remember the concept of friendship as defined in the Bible carries far more meaning than some common definitions used today. Just consider the great mark of friendship that Jesus spoke of to His disciples before He died for them and for us: *"Greater love has no one than this, than to lay down one's life for his friends"* (John 15:13). Because friendship is characterized by selfless, sacrificial love, we can begin to understand John's heart as the friend of the Bridegroom who has at last arrived for His bride. John rejoiced greatly at the Bridegroom's voice, and his joy was complete, because he had long loved the Messiah and yearned for Him to come. John's joy was still greater knowing that the Bridegroom's joy would be fulfilled in finally marrying His bride, His people. Friends rejoice at one another's good fortune, because they long for one another's greatest good. Such is love.

If you are called to be a shepherd in the family of God, then you are called to be the Bridegroom's friend, the best man of sorts. As the best man, your job is to support the establishment of a strong marriage to a good woman who will bless your friend so that His joy might be complete. In His joy, you will find your joy. So your heart for the Bride of Christ must be to help her bring joy to her groom, presenting her as He wishes her to be, in splendor, without blemish or spot or any such thing (Ephesians 5:27). Does that characterize your heart for the Church? Do you love Jesus so much that your singular desire is to see His joy grow through the purification of His bride? These are heavy questions. Don't take them lightly.

They're Watching You

If that is your heart, or at least you and the Holy Spirit within you are striving to see it become so, and if you are confident it is also your calling to shepherd the flock of God, then please consider with me the following passage: *"Shepherd the flock of God which is among you, serving as overseers, not by compulsion but willingly, not for dishonest gain but eagerly; nor as being lords over those entrusted to you, but being examples to the flock; and when the Chief Shepherd appears, you will receive the crown of glory that does not fade away"* (1 Peter 5:2-4). God's Word has much to say here, but let's focus on the last element of Peter's admonition to us: be examples to the flock. Even if you are a shepherd and Jesus's best man, you are yet part of the Bride of Christ. Everything the flock of God is called to obey, you also are called to obey. Everything they are meant to experience of the life of God here on earth, you also are meant to experience. The difference is, you have additional responsibilities because of your *secondary* role as best man, and your role as part of the Bride requires you to exemplify what it is all the other parts are to strive towards.

Are you being that example? Can you say, like Paul, *"Imitate me, just as I also imitate Christ"* (1 Corinthians 11:1)? Would the Bride of Christ around you testify that this is true of you? Would your family say so? If the answer is "no," then you need much, much more time in God's presence. Remember, your only hope of transformation is beholding the glory of your Lord: *"We all, with unveiled face, beholding as in a mirror the glory of the Lord, are being transformed into the same image from glory to glory, just as by the Spirit of the Lord"* (2 Corinthians 3:18). If you're too busy doing the work of the ministry to let this happen, then you are failing in your calling. Your primary call is to *be* a devoted Bride to Christ so that you can be an example to the flock, and from your deep well of spiritual experience, you will be able to draw living water to refresh them.

If your answer to the above questions wasn't what you wish it was, I won't jump to the conclusion that you shouldn't be a shepherd. We have to remember that Paul, who called people to imitate him, also spoke of his struggles: *"For I do not understand my own actions. For I do not do what I want, but I do the very thing I hate. Now if I do what I do not want, I agree with the law, that it is good. So now it is no longer I who do it, but sin that dwells within me. For I know that nothing good dwells in me, that is, in my flesh. For I have the desire to do what is right, but not the ability to carry it out. For I do not do the good I want, but the evil I do not want is what I keep on doing. Now if I do what I do not want, it is no longer I who do it, but sin that dwells within me"* (Romans 7:15-20, ESV). Paul was not immune to the reality of the flesh. The Spirit indeed is willing, but the flesh is weak. He recognizes that alongside the new man who is striving to exemplify the Good Shepherd there is within him also a terrible, destructive sin nature. That sin nature wars against his new creation nature on a regular basis, but the war itself is proof that Paul is a new man. The struggle is proof that Christ now lives in him, and that is his living hope.

So God's Word through Paul keeps us from immediately shrugging off the incredible weight of the calling to live as examples, but it also stops us from leaping off a cliff of despair and leaving the ministry in the face of our imperfect character—*unless* we ought not be shepherds in the first place. The key is found in 1 John 3:7: *"Little children, let no one deceive you. He who practices righteousness is righteous, just as He [Jesus] is righteous."* What is your way of life? Do you *practice* righteousness? Practice, by nature, involves constantly aiming at a goal you have not yet achieved and training yourself to achieve it. If you do not live out everything you strive towards, you should not be surprised. You are no less than the Apostle Paul for your failure. Paul was able to say, *"Not that I have already attained, or am already perfected; but I press on, that I may lay hold of that for which Christ Jesus has also laid hold of me. Brethren, I do not count myself to have apprehended; but one thing I do, forgetting those things which are behind and reaching forward to those things which are ahead, I press toward the goal for the prize of the upward call of God in Christ Jesus."*

What Paul *did* do that was critical was this: He pressed on towards the goal. He *aimed* at being an example for the flock, and he disciplined his body, mind, and spirit to pursue this goal with all His being, because it could mean the difference between life and death for those that followed him. If he represented Christ the Shepherd to them, then when he showed something other than Christ's character, people were being led away from following Christ. He said, *"I discipline my body and bring it into subjection, lest, when I have preached to others, I myself should become disqualified"* (1 Corinthians 9:27). This *is* critical. You do not have to be perfect, but you do have to strive after becoming an example with all your being. This includes your body, pastor. Your body is the temple of the living God, and your lack of self-control over your body is evident to all the flock and leads them astray, causing them to stumble. Give them a better vision of Christ!

This all seems terribly weighty, and it is. Keep in mind that Jesus said, *"whoever causes one of these little ones who believe in Me to sin, it would be better for him if a millstone were hung around his neck, and he were drowned in the depth of the sea. Woe to the world because of offenses! For offenses must come, but woe to that man by whom the offense comes!"* (Matthew 18:6-7). If you lead His little children (His people) astray—especially the actual little ones—then you must realize the terrible judgment that lies ahead of you. Jesus was not simply using exaggerated language for effect; He *is* the Truth, and He only speaks the truth. It really will be better for you to be choked to death and drowned at the bottom of the ocean then to stand before God on the last day as someone who led His people astray by your bad example. You'd have been far better off just serving God outside of leadership positions and working on your own heart rather than trying to lead others.

Can They *See* You?

If, however, you persist in taking the hard road of shepherding others because you can do nothing else as God's call presses upon you, join me in following Paul on a journey of self-discipline for the sake of the Body and Bride of Christ, our Friend and Faithful Bridegroom. What does it mean to be an example to the flock? For one, you have to be *in their view*. People can only follow your example if they can *see* you. How does a child learn to speak? To walk? To connect with other people? They watch their parents—and others. How does a medical student learn to be a good physician? They watch other physicians and join them in the work at hospitals. How do welders learn to weld? They watch someone weld on the job. You get the idea. We all understand that the best way to learn anything is by following someone who has mastered it.

So if you call yourself a shepherd, you are a living example of the Christian life, and people need to see you walking it out. For them to learn to pray, they need to see you praying, and not just in a pulpit, because that isn't realistic for most of them. They need to see you praying for your own needs, being honest and vulnerable before the Father, praying for them and their personal needs when they've had time to really share them with you one-on-one, and praying for others who are dealing with sickness and pain. Jesus's disciples got to see all those things in His life as He ministered to people day after day and as He called them to be with Him in the garden of Gethsemane before His death, pouring out His soul before the Father. If the people are to fight the good fight against the enemies of their souls, they need to see you fight. Men need to be with you as you confess sin and defeat it with the Word of God. They need to see how you do spiritual warfare with worship, Word, and specific prayers to defeat the works of the enemy against your family and your church.

I could go on and on. And you should. You should walk through all the things you wished you saw in the people of your church, the things that your Lord longs to see in His people and that you preach about from the Word of God, and you should ask yourself whether they can see it being lived out in your life. If you don't see it in them, you should question whether you are displaying it at all, and if you know you are, by God's grace, then you need to make sure they can see you doing it, practically. If the way church works is the problem—the structure and tradition of it—then *change it*. The only thing we are bound by when leading God's people is the Word of God, and nothing else matters. If we continue using structures and practices in the church that keep people from experiencing the life of Christ in us and learning to live it themselves, then we are not making disciples, and we are missing the point. We should be willing to reshape *everything* to ensure we make disciples, and that all begins with our visible example as shepherd leaders. As the leader goes, so goes the church.

So we understand that being an example requires visibility and vulnerability. What else does it mean? Ask yourself who it is in your church that is really *devoted* to prayer. You ought to aim to pray that way and more, because you are an example. Who connects well with people, to the point that they pour out their hearts to them? You ought to do so and more. Who teaches well in the church? You should work to see the weight and value of your teaching match and even surpass theirs. This may seem overstated, but the reality is, being an example to others is a high and holy calling. By nature, we ought to be pressing on towards the fullness of Christ Himself, and He is everything that the best members of the Church are and more. Together, they form the fullness of Him, who fills all in all (Ephesians 1:23). In fact, because of this reality that each part is unique and necessary, we can accept that some parts will be naturally better examples of certain elements of Christ's nature than we are, and we should celebrate that in them, not envy it. However, that does not change the reality that we are to *strive* to be examples in every way to the flock. It should be our goal to be the closest to Jesus and most obedient to His Word in every area so that whenever anyone comes to us in need, we can show them the way of Christ from real experience with the Living God.

Being an example to the flock will require drastic changes in lifestyle. If we tend to get up a bit late because we spent too much time on entertainment the night before, then we will have to set as many alarms as it takes and cut whatever it takes to get up early and seek the Father for ourselves, our families, the Church, and His glory. If that entertainment tends to corrupt our spirit and keep us from connecting with God, we need to bow before Him in repentance and genuinely change our ways, renewing a covenant to allow nothing evil before our eyes and to devote ourselves to love Him rather than the world. If we chase after money in any area of life, we must put that to death with the crucified past life and choose to serve God rather than money, for no one can serve two masters. If we only read the Word to preach, but we expect our congregation to read it for enjoyment and personal obedience and connection with God, then we need to overhaul our time in the Scriptures and train ourselves to go after the Father's heart. If we show a tremendous lack of self-control in what we consume, to the point that it shows physically and labels us as hypocrites when we teach on cultivating the fruit of the Spirit, then we need to cut off and throw away whatever it takes to serve as examples of a disciplined life. If we think of ourselves as "not a people person," we have to take that thought captive in obedience to Christ who came to earth entirely for people and sent us on mission in life entirely for people. The same goes for those who spend time with people all the time but are not willing to proclaim the glory of God through preaching His Word in authority and power. God can change a man's nature. If we don't believe that, then what are we doing in ministry?

Selfish Shepherds Will Be Removed

Let's take a look at one more section of Scripture before we allow ourselves to rest on God's grace in Christ (which, praise God, is freely available to us all). Go to Ezekiel 34:1-10:

> *"And the word of the Lord came to me, saying, 'Son of man, prophesy against the shepherds of Israel, prophesy and say to them, 'Thus says the Lord God to the shepherds: 'Woe to the shepherds of Israel who feed themselves! Should not the shepherds feed the flocks? You eat the fat and clothe yourselves with the*

> wool; you slaughter the fatlings, but you do not feed the flock. The weak you have not strengthened, nor have you healed those who were sick, nor bound up the broken, nor brought back what was driven away, nor sought what was lost; but with force and cruelty you have ruled them. So they were scattered because there was no shepherd; and they became food for all the beasts of the field when they were scattered. My sheep wandered through all the mountains, and on every high hill; yes, My flock was scattered over the whole face of the earth, and no one was seeking or searching for them.' Therefore, you shepherds, hear the word of the Lord: 'As I live,' says the Lord God, 'surely because My flock became a prey, and My flock became food for every beast of the field, because there was no shepherd, nor did My shepherds search for My flock, but the shepherds fed themselves and did not feed My flock'— therefore, O shepherds, hear the word of the Lord! Thus says the Lord God: 'Behold, I am against the shepherds, and I will require My flock at their hand; I will cause them to cease feeding the sheep, and the shepherds shall feed themselves no more; for I will deliver My flock from their mouths, that they may no longer be food for them.'

Don't gloss over this. What God said to those who called themselves shepherds in ancient Israel applies to us who go by that name today, because God never changes, and His heart towards His people and their proper care does not change. So, please, for God's sake and the Church's sake, allow this Word to have its full effect on you and anyone you're grooming to lead. What's the main message here? God is deeply grieved over the pitiful state of His people, and He's so tired of selfish shepherds who spend more time on themselves than on taking care of the pressing needs of His people that He is ready to remove them from their positions. Who is to blame for all of this? Specifically, shepherds who feed themselves. Could that, in any way, be you?

Do you serve the Church *primarily* to take care of yourself or even your own family? It's right and good to provide for your family, in fact, it's a biblical command Paul gave to Timothy. It's right and good for a messenger of the Gospel to earn their living by the work of the Gospel. However, that has nothing to do with the call. A man is called to serve Jesus as a shepherd of His people completely independent of any promise of financial provision in return for service. If you had nowhere to lay your head as you followed Jesus, you would still be called, and you'd be no different than the early disciples. If you were starved and homeless, you'd just be resonating with the Apostle Paul who experienced both as he followed Christ—and he deliberately worked a trade in order to present the Gospel free of charge as well. Money has *nothing* to do with your call.

If you feel that it does, and especially if you feel as though you were "hired" to do the "job" of preaching, teaching, or soul-care/counseling, then you have no place leading the people of

God until that changes. What did Jesus say? *"I am the good shepherd. The good shepherd gives His life for the sheep. But a hireling, he who is not the shepherd, one who does not own the sheep, sees the wolf coming and leaves the sheep and flees; and the wolf catches the sheep and scatters them. The hireling flees because he is a hireling and does not care about the sheep"* (John 10:11-13). If shepherding is simply your job, then you don't truly care about the sheep. You are feeding yourself, and God is coming against you to remove you from your position. Jesus, on the other hand, is the Good Shepherd. He cares for the sheep. And those who are truly called to shepherd the flock of God are called to display the image of the Good Shepherd and to lay down their lives for the sheep. They care so much that they'd sacrifice their personal desires and needs for the sake of the sheep, as Jesus and Paul did.

Putting Commitment to the Test

If you believe you are trying to fulfill a shepherd's call out of a good heart, then let the rest of the passage test that commitment. God said to these shepherds: *"The weak you have not strengthened, nor have you healed those who were sick, nor bound up the broken, nor brought back what was driven away, nor sought what was lost; but with force and cruelty you have ruled them. So they were scattered because there was no shepherd; and they became food for all the beasts of the field when they were scattered. My sheep wandered through all the mountains, and on every high hill; yes, My flock was scattered over the whole face of the earth, and no one was seeking or searching for them."* So apply that to your ministry. Have you strengthened the weak? This isn't asking if you've taught things that may or may not have strengthened people in the audience here and there. It's asking whether you have discerned who among the flock appear to have no strength to stand with God for their families and for others, and *strengthened* them, taking them from that place of weakness to a place of greater strength with discernible fruit in their lives that you can observe because you really *know* them. Can some of them now offer strength to others from the wellspring they've gained from you?

Have you healed the sick or bound up the broken? Churches are chock-full of terribly broken people who have been through the ringer and come out the other side unsure of how to stand. They have wounds upon wounds that are spiritual and emotional as well as, sometimes, physical. Do you know this about the people in your church? Not in the general sense, either. Do you know what they're dealing with because they've told you, and you've listened, time and again? Do you know the things that keep them up at night and that drive them to do most of what they do day to day? Do you also know their sins because you've given them space to confess their sins to you or others so that you all might pray for them that they might be healed? If the answer isn't a resounding "yes," then something needs to change in the way you "do" church and life as the Body of Christ. A Body can only weep and rejoice as one if the different parts share a common experience, if they know what is going on with one another and endure it together.

Do you go after the strays? When people leave the church, do you pursue them so they can be certain of the Father's pursuing love and so you can be certain wherever they are going is going to lead them to the abundant life Jesus offers? Do you leave the church walls to find the strays that you are sure have walked away from God? Do you reach out to the lost who have never claimed Christ? Remember, Timothy, to do the work of an evangelist and fulfill your ministry. What's more, Jesus sent you as the Father sent Him, and He came to seek and to save what was lost, so we must do the same. If we don't do these things, then the people end up scattered. They end up as prey for the "wild beasts," the beasts of the kingdom of Satan and this world that long to steal, kill, and destroy. These people will suffer, and it will be our fault. Do you see the poor state of the Church today? Much of it could be avoided with good shepherds following after Jesus's heart.

So let's take stock. Having gone through this chapter, all of us who believe we are called to shepherd God's flock ought to have arrived at one of two conclusions. You could be a called shepherd who is serving as well as anyone can with the sin nature that wars against us, and you simply need to pursue the Good Shepherd's heart yet more by binding up the wounded, strengthening the weak, and going after the strayed and lost, pressing further into

Christ to become further conformed to His image. You may even find that you're failing to a point, and it's simply because you are doing the work alone, in which case you need to look around you for the elders/shepherds God has placed near you who need to be appointed, given permission, and charged to do what they are being called to do. No man is meant to shepherd the flock of God alone. That model is a product of a religious culture that misses the picture presented in New Testament Christianity.

Alternately, you could have realized you truly do not reflect the Good Shepherd well at all, and you are either not ready or not called to this role in the Body of Christ. If this is true of you, gather some *good* men around you who can help you walk through this season, and confess your sins to them, asking them to pray that you might be healed. Then, submit to the biblical counsel available through God's Word, asking them to hold you accountable to walking it out. You may very well need to leave ministerial leadership until a time when your character is fit for the shepherd's call, so as to save both yourself and your hearers from great heartache and judgement. And if you realize that this entire ministry path in your life has been self-serving, you ought to get as far from leadership roles as you can and as close to Jesus as you can, testing yourself to see whether you are in the faith. It is the humble who God visits and helps. Those who recognize their deep sin debt and need for Christ are those who receive mercy and find grace to help in time of need. It takes repentance and faith to be born again into the family of God. If you have been a wolf in sheep's clothing in any sense, you need to take full hold of the grace available to you in Jesus Christ and start over as a newborn in the Kingdom of God.

In the end, the only hope we have is Jesus, the Living Hope, who promises to fill every one of His true shepherds with His Spirit to enable them to live the high and holy calling placed upon their life. Like Paul, we can run the good race *"striving according to His working which works in me mightily,"* (Col. 1:29), and it can be our *"earnest expectation and hope that in nothing I shall be ashamed, but with all boldness, as always, so now also Christ will be magnified in my body, whether by life or by death"* (Philippians 1:20).

Prayer Response

A prayer of examination:

"Jesus, I long to be a good friend to you when you come for your Bride. I long to care about what you care about. I want to represent your heart here and now. Have I been a faithful shepherd of your people, or do you see someone who has missed your heart? Is my deceitful heart in any way making me live like a hired hand who feeds himself and neglects the sheep? I trust you to refine me in your fire and reveal my true intentions. Move me to repentance in every way I need it, and help me to become a good steward of the mystery of the gospel."

A prayer of repentance and faith:

"Father, I have lied. I have claimed to be a shepherd when, in reality, I have had none of Jesus's heart for His people. I have done pastoral work and used people to feed the needs of my own soul for accomplishment, for purpose, and for financial gain. I have not bound up the injured, strengthened the weak, or gone after the strayed. I have left them to die without help while I carried on with business as usual, 'maintaining the organization.' For that, I repent. Jesus, please cover my sins with your blood, and make me righteous."

Chapter 11

The Ancient Way

"Thus says the Lord: 'Stand by the roads, and look, and ask for the ancient paths, where the good way is; and walk in it, and find rest for your souls.'"— Jeremiah 6:16, ESV

THE BIBLE ENDS WITH A TALE OF TWO WOMEN. Starting with Revelation 17 and continuing on through the last chapters of the book, God presents two pictures of beauty: that of the world, and that of His kingdom, and He personifies them to help us understand. It begins with a prostitute. *"I saw a woman sitting on a scarlet beast which was full of names of blasphemy, having seven heads and ten horns. The woman was arrayed in purple and scarlet, and adorned with gold and precious stones and pearls, having in her hand a golden cup full of abominations and the filthiness of her fornication. And on her forehead a name was written: Mystery, Babylon the Great, the mother of harlots and of the abominations of the earth"* (Revelation 17:3-5).

Here we have the first lady, clearly one that God the Father would not choose to give to His Son. However, were it not for the mention of beasts, blasphemy, and unfaithfulness, I imagine most people would be rather impressed by her. She'd wear only the best, her frame draped in a custom-made designer dress, her neck, wrists, and fingers festooned with priceless jewelry, and she'd have a cup of the finest aged wine in her hand, carrying herself with confidence, the envy of all. The rest of her story makes it clear that the whole world was besotted with her, as the Word says, *"...all the nations have drunk of the wine of the wrath of her fornication, the kings of the earth have committed fornication with her, and the merchants of the earth have become rich through the abundance of her luxury"* (Revelation 18:3). Truly, most people had been fooled by what they could see.

So where is the other lady? *"And I heard, as it were, the voice of a great multitude, as the sound of many waters and as the sound of mighty thunderings, saying, 'Alleluia! For the Lord God Omnipotent reigns! Let us be glad and rejoice and give Him glory, for the marriage of the Lamb has come, and His wife has made herself ready.' And to her it was granted to be arrayed in fine linen, clean and bright, for the fine linen is the righteous acts of the saints*" (Revelation 19:6-8). What a stark contrast! The first woman is bedecked from head to toe with costly, eye-catching attire, making a show of what a good time she will have with her wine and revelry, but she stands on the eve of judgment. And the second is simply clothed in clean, bright linen with no other descriptors given, and she rejoices beyond measure in her Groom. Notably, it is the second woman who is described as having "made herself ready."

Read the next passage back-to-back with Revelation 19:8 above. The previous chapter of Revelation ended Lady Babylon's narrative with a confrontation for her sins and a day of terrible judgment; her lovers looked on as she faced destruction, saying, "*Alas, alas, that great city that was clothed in fine linen, purple, and scarlet, and adorned with gold and precious stones and pearls! For in one hour such great riches came to nothing*'" (Revelation 18:16-17). Well would you look at that? She, too is clothed in fine linen. Both ladies try to wear something nice for their lovers, so what's the difference? *Heart*. Lady Babylon has strived, schemed, connived, fornicated, and bought her expensive clothing at the price of her soul, as Jesus said, "*what will it profit a man if he gains the whole world, and loses his own soul?*" (Mark 8:36). She earned what she had, and she did it for herself. In the end, she will have nothing, and it will be her own doing.

The Bride, too, has made an effort for her lover, as the Word says, "*the marriage of the Lamb has come, and His wife has made herself ready*" (Revelation 19:7). She has made herself ready, but how did she do it? It says it was *granted* to her to clothe herself in fine linen. The privilege of being clothed is given to her by another. The Bride has nothing except that it be provided by her Beloved. He is her Provider, and she can gain nothing for herself. The position of the Bride is one of complete dependence upon the one she loves, and her trust for Him is what allows her to receive what she needs to clothe herself. This distinction is critical. Consider this parable Jesus shared with the religious leaders and respected people of Israel: "*The kingdom of heaven is like a certain king who arranged a marriage for his son and sent out his servants to call those who were invited to the wedding...But when the king came in to see the guests, he saw a man there who did not have on a wedding garment. So he said to him, 'Friend, how did you come in here without a wedding garment?' And he was speechless. Then the king said to the servants, 'Bind him hand and foot, take him away, and cast him into outer darkness; there will be weeping and gnashing of teeth' For many are called but few are chosen*" (Matthew 22:2, 11-14). Jesus makes it clear here that some people—probably those like his audience, the religious folk—would try to come to the wedding feast without wedding garments on. They would wear what they had bought themselves through their hard work, expecting that they would be accepted. But the King will not accept them as they stand by their own merit. No, he will only accept them if they are clothed in wedding garments which He provides and which they are chosen to receive. It's all about the Bride's heart, just as the Word says to all godly women, *"Do not let your adornment be merely outward...rather let it be the hidden person of the heart..."* (1 Peter 3:3-4).

So, we need clothes for the wedding day, and we need them to be provided by Jesus, but what does that say about how to get them? After all, the Scripture *does* say that the Bride is allowed to clothe *herself*, and the fine linen is the righteous deeds of the saints. Guess what? She's a saint. Yes, however, these truths—clothing oneself and being provided with clothes by another—are not mutually exclusive, just as the twin realities that we are saved by faith in Christ's work alone and that we must keep working towards Christlikeness are not mutually exclusive. The truth is, someone can buy me clothes, and I can put them on, but someone can also buy me fabric, and I can make clothing (if I learn the skill), then put them on. Someone can also teach me to make them with the fabric they've given me. In the case of these linen wedding garments of righteousness, we can look to the Gospel. Christ's righteous standing before the Father is a free gift provided by God to us when we put our faith in the Son.

We get to be *clothed* in the righteousness of Christ by faith: *"I will greatly rejoice in the Lord; my soul shall be joyful in my God, for He has clothed me with the garments of salvation; he has covered me with the robe of righteousness, as a bridegroom decks himself with ornaments, and as a bride adorns herself with her jewels"* (Isaiah 61:10). As we prepare to stand before our Groom at the wedding feast, we have the promise of clothing ourselves in the robes of righteousness He provides, and His perfect life living within us empowers us to clothe ourselves in righteous deeds. On their own, the things we do would amount to filthy rags for our wedding day, but *in Christ*, those deeds become pure white garments of grace as we are presented in splendor, without blemish or spot. The Word of God urges us to trust this reality by faith, and to express that faith through works done *for* Jesus in righteousness. We can cultivate a lifestyle of such works by practicing the wisdom given by Apostle Paul: *"Put on the Lord Jesus Christ, and make no provision for the flesh, to fulfill its lusts"* (Romans 13:14). We must give no place to the flesh, the old life of self-centered works, as we take who Jesus is and what He has done and hide ourselves in that identity. Then, we may discover what Paul discovered, that *"to live is Christ, and to die is gain"* (Phil. 1:21).

Two Kingdom Cities

As we look at the two women represented in Revelation 19, the surrounding context quickly shows us that they also represent two cities: Babylon and Jerusalem. Revelation 21 kicks off with a vision of the second city: *"Now I saw a new heaven and a new earth, for the first heaven and the first earth had passed away. Also there was no more sea. Then I, John, saw the holy city, New Jerusalem, coming down out of heaven from God, prepared as a bride adorned for her husband. And I heard a loud voice from heaven saying, 'Behold, the tabernacle of God is with men, and He will dwell with them, and they shall be His people. God Himself will be with them and be their God'"* (Revelation 21:1-3). This beautiful moment at the end of the age is the consummation of Christ's covenant with His bride, the Church. The wedding supper is finished, and they are at last united in holy matrimony, forever to be together. John describes the bride here as a city, fulfilling Jesus's words spoken to His disciples during the Sermon on the Mount, *"You are the light of the world. A city that is set on a hill cannot be hidden. Nor do they light a lamp and put it under a basket, but on a lampstand, and it gives light to all who are in the house. Let your light so shine before men, that they may see your good works and glorify your Father in heaven"* (Matthew 5:14-16).

Throughout this sermon, Jesus is describing the character of His Father's Kingdom. Keep in mind that at this time, the "gospel of the kingdom" Jesus preached was good news of God's rule and reign being available to people *before* Jesus had finished His work to secure mankind's entry into that kingdom. They weren't hearing about His life, death, and resurrection. They were just hearing about the life available to them through covenant with God Almighty, a covenant they would soon find they could only keep through Jesus's life, death, and resurrection. This kingdom is represented by a city, just as the kingdom of Satan, the "ruler of this world," (John 12:31) is represented by the city of Babylon in Revelation. In each case, the cities embody the values of their kingdoms and the character of their rulers. We see that the new Jerusalem coming down from heaven in Revelation 21 is clearly going to perfectly represent God's kingdom and character as He promises to dwell there with them. The chapter goes on to say that there will be no need for the light of lamp or sun, because the Lord God will be their light. That city will shine brighter than anything has since the beginning of time. But Jesus said to His disciples in His sermon two thousand years ago that *they* were *then* the light of the world and a city on a hill.

The church He was starting would already shine the light of God into the world through His presence within them, as He promised, *"If anyone loves Me, he will keep My word; and My Father will love him, and We will come to him and make Our home with him"* (John 14:23). The kingdom breaks into the world now through God coming to dwell within man. The church really *is* the fullness of Jesus Christ who fills all in all (Ephesians 1:23), but the work of sin in our flesh creates a barrier to the full inbreaking of the kingdom of God through Jesus dwelling within us. God's people *can* hide their light now, though they won't on the last day. That's why Jesus urges us in the sermon *not* to hide our light under a basket but to put it on a stand so that it gives light to all in the house. The Church has to live as a unified city with its own kingdom culture counter to the world and take its stand on a hill in view of all. There, it must shine the light of the Gospel of truth, exposing the dark deeds of the world so that all might repent and turn to the King of Kings. Just as any city is known by the common character of its citizens, to the point that certain groups of people living counter-culturally can give a city a bad reputation, so it is that the kingdom culture of this city on a hill is expressed in the character of each citizen, each member of the Body and Bride of Christ. Jesus's sermon helps people understand the character demonstrated by true citizens of this kingdom city. They are meek, not demanding their own way, holding their will in check. They are forgiving, keeping no records of wrongs done against them. They watch what they say and keep their commitments, because God within them *always* keeps His Word. And they suffer willingly with and for their Lord and His kingdom.

It is this last quality that causes the church to stand out so clearly in contrast with the worldly city of Babylon in the final chapters of the Bible: shared suffering with a suffering Savior. As Babylon's judgment comes, God speaks these words: *"Come out of her, my people, lest you share in her sins, and lest you receive of her plagues. For her sins have reached to heaven, and God has remembered her iniquities. Render to her just as she rendered to you, and repay her double according to her works; in the cup which she has mixed, mix double for her. In the measure that she glorified herself and lived luxuriously, in the same measure give her torment and sorrow..."* (Revelation 19:4-7). This city is judged for having lived *luxuriously* and glorified *herself*; she sought every possible comfort in life through greed and

160

sexuality and did her best to make herself great in the eyes of others. God calls His people to separate completely from this terrible city, pitting her way of life *directly against* the way of life of God's people inhabiting the new Jerusalem and the way they are to represent that kingdom now as a city on a hill. Christ's Bride, the church, is not to seek comfort in this life, and they are not to live for themselves. They are not to build their own kingdoms here on earth to give themselves glory. They exist for the sole purpose of glorifying the Almighty God above all things, the embodiment of truth and justice, the one for whom and by whom all things were created!

Together Through It All

And they suffer for it. When Revelation introduces the marriage supper of the Lamb—that climax moment of history—it comes at the end of a period of near unbearable suffering for those believers living during the period of the great tribulation. Revelation 19 begins: "*After these things I heard a loud voice of a great multitude in heaven, saying, 'Alleluia! Salvation and glory and honor and power belong to the Lord our God! For true and righteous are His judgments, because He has judged the great harlot who corrupted the earth with her fornication; and He has avenged on her the blood of His servants shed by her'...'Let us be glad and rejoice and give Him glory, for the marriage of the Lamb has come, and His wife has made herself ready*'" (Revelation 19:1-7). To our ears, celebrating the destruction of sin city probably sounds like a pretty gruesome way to spend your wedding day, but we haven't been through what they've been through. These saints in heaven just witnessed the horrific slaughter of their loved ones by beheading for the last months and years, each day watching people who had lived holy, selfless lives be confronted by godless men and killed for no other cause than loyalty: they refused to bow the knee to anyone but Jesus. Because of their devotion, a world full of people who hate God turned against them, and the saints gave their lives for their Lord. So, to see this terrible city at last face judgment, to know she will no more oversee the destruction of the innocent, is certainly a cause for rejoicing. It's like Jews who heard that Hitler and the Nazis had been defeated and the few of them who were left could at last live in peace without the threat of death and imprisonment haunting them day and night. They'd have breathed a long, labored sigh of relief, and joy would have risen up inside them like a fountain until it burst in a shout of praise! At last, the enemy was defeated. The years of suffering and constant battle with fear were over. Justice had won! Now that peace had been bought with a price, a feast could happen. A beautiful marriage could begin that would continue for eternity without threat of fear, pain, or death. Nothing would disturb this magnificent union. Together, the bride and Groom could rest.

    So the new, beautiful city of Jerusalem forms through suffering. They get to dwell with God and rejoice in His kindness poured out on them forever because they suffered with Him for a short time on earth. Suffering now, glory later. This has always been the heart cry of God's people. When Jesus began His ministry, what did He say to His disciples? *"Blessed are those who are persecuted for righteousness' sake, for theirs is the kingdom of heaven. Blessed are you when they revile and persecute you, and say all kinds of evil against you falsely for My sake. Rejoice and be exceedingly glad, for great is your reward in heaven, for so they persecuted the prophets who were before you"* (Matthew 5:10-12). You will be blessed—you will receive good things, worthy rewards from God—when you are treated badly for standing with Jesus. This is part of following Him. Before He went to the cross, He shared with His disciples what they might expect after He was gone: *"Remember the word that I said to you, 'A servant is not greater than his master.' If they persecuted Me, they will also persecute you"* (John 15:20. To go where Jesus goes, we must walk the same path and share the same struggles. We are not greater than Him; we shouldn't receive better treatment. Jesus also said, *"If **anyone** desires to come after Me, let him deny himself, and take up his cross, and follow Me. For whoever desires to save his life will lose it, but whoever loses his life for My sake will find it"* (Matthew 16:24-25). In case any of us thought that maybe this would not apply to us, that perhaps just the early disciples or people called to be prophets or missionaries might deal with these things—but not *us*—Jesus made the matter clear. Anyone who wants to "come after Him"—and I guarantee you that you *do* want to come after Him if you want to get to heaven, as that's where He went—must expect to lose their life for His sake. *And* they must be willing to deny themselves, to become self-less. The Bride of Christ pictured in Revelation understood this. God's people enduring the tribulation knew they had to be willing to suffer with Jesus in order to be glorified with Him. They knew they had to deny themselves the things their flesh wanted now, in this life, in order to receive everything promised to them in the next. Babylon, in contrast, represented all those who decided they needed their best life now, those who were unwilling to choose suffering and selflessness because they wanted what they could get for themselves in this short time allotted to them before eternity. What a terrible trade they made.

But the Bride—she's different. She can wait for that wedding day, knowing that keeping herself from other lovers until that time might be painful and at times lonely, but it's worth it for the committed groom and beautiful ending to her story which await. And she has always been this way. People from long before Jesus were making the choice of losing their lives for His sake, were choosing suffering now for glory later. Just read Hebrews 11. From the beginning to the end, that chapter shares the amazing journeys of people of faith who chose to trust God for things they could not see, though in so doing they gave up much of what they could see and for which they could have lived instead. *"These all died in faith, not having received the promises, but having seen them afar off were assured of them, embraced them and confessed that they were strangers and pilgrims on the earth. For those who say such things declare plainly that they seek a homeland. And truly if they had called to mind that country from which they had come out, they would have had opportunity to return. But now they desire a better, that is, a heavenly country. Therefore God is not ashamed to be called their God, for He has prepared a city for them"* (Hebrews 11:13-16). They lived for another world. Every person called righteous in the Old Testament had to make this choice. This was the ancient way.

Strangers and Exiles

"Thus says the Lord: 'Stand by the roads, and look, and ask for the ancient paths, where the good way is; and walk in it, and find rest for your souls'" (Jeremiah 6:16). When God's people had begun to serve themselves and false gods to the point that they received judgment from a foreign nation in order to discipline them back into repentance, that was God's Word to them. Return to the ancient path. There you will find rest. And from the very beginning of the Church that Jesus built, God's people followed this ancient way. They saw themselves as strangers and exiles on the earth, waiting for a better city, as Paul encouraged the Church in Philippi, *"...our citizenship is in heaven, from which we also eagerly wait for the Savior, the Lord Jesus Christ, who will transform our lowly body that it may be conformed to His glorious body..."* (Philippians 3:20-21). They lived for new Jerusalem long before it came. They

waited, *really waited*, for Jesus. They were ready for their master whenever He might return. They lived as though eternity was knocking!

The Church started with a bang as thousands got saved during Peter's first sermon after Jesus's resurrection, and they began to live in loving community with people getting saved *daily*, but even so the Church quickly discovered the truth of Jesus's admonition about persecution. Both the Jews and Rome became their sworn enemies, and the happy family of God had to disperse across the then-known world. *But that did not destroy their spirit.* Peter writes to those early believers who had scattered from persecution, saying, *"Beloved, do not think it strange concerning the fiery trial which is to try you, as though some strange thing happened to you; but rejoice to the extent that you partake of Christ's sufferings, that when His glory is revealed, you may also be glad with exceeding joy. If you are reproached for the name of Christ, blessed are you, for the Spirit of glory and of God rests upon you. On their part He is blasphemed, but on your part He is glorified"* (1 Peter 4:12-14). He doesn't want them to let their flesh trick them into believing they deserve better or that they are somehow especially miserable due to their personal trials. No! They are to understand that this is their heritage, to suffer with Jesus now and be glorified with Him later. The joy that is to come is worth exceedingly abundantly more than anything they could ever face now. Truly, *"...the sufferings of this present time are not worthy to be compared with the glory which shall be revealed in us"*

(Romans 8:18).

Not only did the early Church understand this, but the wider Body of Christ around the world does even today. The uniquely comfortable position we in Western nations (the U.S. especially) have occupied in recent centuries is not in any way "normal" for the historic church. God's people were never intended to live in a way so *different* from the way of Jesus. He walked a road marked with suffering and exhibited great joy as He endured it because He knew what was coming at the end, and He knew what He had in His Father's presence in the here and now. In the same way, those who choose to follow Jesus in Muslim-majority nations today understand that they are choosing to lose their lives rather than save them. They know that once they say "yes" to the Gospel, they are saying "no" to everything they've ever known, to their communities, to business connections, to opportunity, to their families, and possibly to the privilege of breathing. When those believers are baptized, the chance that they will not only die with Christ spiritually and symbolically but *actually* die with Him physically is very high, because their culture's belief system teaches that leaving their former faith is deserving of death, and it is considered honorable for another person to enforce that penalty. The honor usually falls to family members. So when they read the gospel of Luke where Jesus says, *"You will be betrayed even by parents and brothers, relatives and friends; and they will put some of you to death. And you will be hated by all for My name's sake"* (Luke 21:16-17), they actually expect that to happen, and they weigh their decisions and level of commitment to Christ based on the expectancy that His words will at some point prove true—unlike those of us in the Western world who gloss right over such passages due to our complete inability to comprehend them. Because we do this, we often *miss out on* the genuine presence of God coming to dwell within us by faith and empower us to live a life of supernatural endurance. Since we don't expect to need that, He does not provide it, and we do not experience it. The next time you wonder why the Church today doesn't look much like the early Church, consider how easy we've made it to join the Church. We have practically said, "choose Jesus; just bring Him on board with what you've got going on, being prepared to change a little bit, and He will help you get everything you need to be happy," or, alternately, "Jesus isn't *really* interested in the things you're doing with your life, He's about religion, so just do church, and He'll be happy with you, then you can do everything else that really matters to you the rest of the week and leave Him out of it."

This thought process can't even *exist* for historic Christian communities in the Middle East such as Iran. In that country, Christians live in hiding, worshipping in abandoned buildings or private homes, sharing their faith discreetly while always wondering, "will this person reveal to others that I am a Christian? Will my family be safe after today?" They have to hide their Bibles and whisper when they meet a curious friend at the coffee shop. Then we have brethren all across Africa in places like Sudan and Nigeria who fear leaving their families to work because rampaging terrorist groups like Boko Haram roam the countryside looking for Christian communities to rob and burn to the ground. These men may come home to find their wives or children raped and murdered. It isn't only Muslim-majority nations where we see this marked difference in Christianity either, though such nations account for a *huge* segment of the world's population today—somewhere between one quarter and one third of the earth's total. You might even think it's simply the poor, uneducated nations whose citizens think and act so brutally. Think twice. China's economy is second only to that of the United States, not to mention their significant advances in technology due to a thriving and rigorous educational system. Yet, they imprison Christian pastors on a regular basis just for preaching the truth *privately*, and tens of millions of Christians in that country must gather in secret and often at night in order to avoid being shut down. Church buildings have been condemned and destroyed, and those who wish to worship publicly must submit to Communist-sanctioned church systems that operate under strict control and often deny core doctrines such as the deity of Christ. For *countless* Christian brethren across the world (probably more than the entire population of the United States) the Christian life is a trade—suffering now for glory later: self-denial here and now for God's kindness forever after.

This ancient way is *our heritage*. The true Church is one that suffers with Jesus willingly and with joy because they know that their real life is hidden with Christ in God. They believe that nothing on this earth can truly hurt them, because they have eternal life waiting for them. They can turn the world upside down, and the gates of hell cannot prevail against them, because they have nothing to lose and have already won Jesus their prize. And I'm here to tell you, *we can be that again!* The Church in the West does not have to give up and die, though it most certainly will die if we don't change. No Church dies without God's permission, but in the Revelation letters to the churches, we see that Jesus is crystal clear: "repent, or I will remove your place. Your lamp will be put out." This doesn't have to be our fate. In this critical hour of the world, the Western Church has a chance to change. And it begins with a change in perspective.

Prayer Response

"Lord Jesus, thank you for making it possible for me to come to your marriage supper. On my own, I could never get in. I would have only the filthy rags of my own righteousness. But because of your work, I can enter with robes of purest white! Give me the privilege of clothing myself in your righteousness, and teach me to live now in such a way that I obey your command to 'let my light shine before men.' Like Paul said you did within him, work powerfully within me to will and to do for your good pleasure. Do great deeds of selfless love that show others you are alive in me. Purge my life of all that belongs to this world. I want to be as far from Babylon as possible, and I want no part of it, even if it makes life easier. Test me, and let the fire leave nothing but a new man. I want to follow the ancient way. Renew my mind to think like brethren of old, and strengthen me to follow their path of shared suffering and enduring hope."

Chapter 12

Heritage of Hope

"Blessed be the God and Father of our Lord Jesus Christ! According to his great mercy, he has caused us to be born again to a living hope through the resurrection of Jesus Christ from the dead." — 1 Peter 1:3, ESV

How do we do it, then? After catching a glimpse of such a glorious vision for the Church in the previous chapter, we are left wondering how on earth we might recover and realize such a vision. The answer is simple: we look to Jesus. *"...let us lay aside every weight, and the sin which so easily ensnares us, and let us run with endurance the race that is set before us, looking unto Jesus, the author and finisher of our faith, who for the joy that was set before Him endured the cross, despising the shame, and has sat down at the right hand of the throne of God"* (Hebrews 12:1b-2). It is possible to run this race of life better and farther only by looking to the one who successfully ran the race: our Lord and Savior, our Beloved, Jesus Christ. He did it, and He did it well. He won the race! And lest we think we can learn nothing from this because we aren't God, we must remember that He did it *as a man*. He was the second Adam, the one who did right what Adam did wrong while facing Adam's fleshly weaknesses. The Christian life can be lived because Jesus lived it for us and lives it now *in us*. So we must look to Him for the way to walk the ancient path. How did He do it? He had His eyes *fixed* ahead. When Paul wrote his letter to the Church at Philippi, he urged them to *"let this mind be in you which was also in Christ Jesus,"* (Philippians 2:5), and the letter goes on to describe what it looks like to have the mind of Christ. It looks like selflessness, obedience, suffering, and glory. In this passage, we see what the mind of Christ accomplished, but what was *on* His mind to make that happen? Hebrews 12:2 reveals that it was joy. He had His mind on the prize. And what was the prize? Listen to this prophecy about Jesus from the prophet Isaiah:

> *"...He was cut off from the land of the living; for the transgressions of My people He was stricken...Yet it pleased the Lord to bruise Him; He has put Him to grief. When You [the*

Father] make His [the Son's] soul an offering for sin, He shall see His offspring, He shall prolong His days, And the pleasure of the Lord shall prosper in His hand. He shall see the labor of His soul, and be satisfied. By His knowledge My righteous Servant shall justify many, for He shall bear their iniquities. Therefore I will divide Him a portion with the great, and He shall divide the spoil with the strong, because He poured out His soul unto death, and He was numbered with the transgressors, and He bore the sin of many, and made intercession for the transgressors." – Isaiah 53:8-12, addition mine.

What Hope Looks Like

In this passage, God shares His heart about the cross and reveals some of the mind of Christ that was driving Him as He ran His race and finished His work. When Jesus's soul made an offering for sin, His eyes were fixed on His reward. He saw His offspring—all the countless men and women who will inherit His kingdom as co-heirs at the end of the age by faith—and He was satisfied. It was *worth it* to Him to endure everything He had to face in order to rescue a family for Himself to whom He could show His kindness forever in love. Because He did this great work, God the Father raised Him up and gave Him a place of highest honor. What's amazing to me is that it says He would divide the spoil with others who would have their own places of honor, and that means us—people who are adopted into the Father's family through identification with the Son by faith. He was looking forward to a reward which is in many ways *equal* to the reward we can hope to receive as redeemed children of God. Wow!

That is how the early Christians once managed and how today's persecuted brethren manage to live lives of endurance and rejoicing through suffering. Their selfless lives shine like stars in the midst of their crooked and twisted generations. They have *hope*. And this is where the rubber meets the road. This is where we get some freedom and a measure of victory for our individual walk with Christ, which is critical, because the Body is made of many members, and as the members go, so goes the Body. The Church of God on earth is only able to glorify Him insomuch as the members individually glorify Him together. Let's consider what God says about hope:

> *"Therefore, having been justified by faith, we have peace with God through our Lord Jesus Christ, through whom also we have access by faith into this grace in which we stand, and rejoice in hope of the glory of God. And not only that, but we also glory in tribulations, knowing that tribulation produces perseverance; and perseverance, character; and character, hope. Now hope does not disappoint, because the love of God has been poured out in our hearts by the Holy Spirit who was given to us"* (Romans 5:1-5).

We live at peace with God. Stop and try to grasp that, just a moment. The Living God and Judge of the Earth—a Consuming

Fire that destroys all adversaries and hates wickedness—has wrath stored up to obliterate all sources of evil so that His kingdom of purity and righteousness can reign forever afterwards. He has appointed a day to judge the earth, and it is coming soon. But *we* are at peace with Him. We are on *His* side, if our faith truly rests in Jesus and His finished work alone. Nothing can make Him turn against us anymore, because we are one with Him now, and He dwells within us. He has made us His home. Peace! And as if that was not enough to marvel at forever, the Word says we "rejoice in hope of the glory of God." If we understand this in light of the whole of Scripture, I believe we will see this can mean two things: we rejoice as we wait for God to be glorified, fully revealed in all His infinite majesty and worshipped for Who He is as He has always deserved, AND we rejoice as we expect a day to come when we ourselves will be glorified as Jesus was in His resurrection Body and we will share in God's own glory, something He had promised to *never share* with anyone other than Himself but which He can now share with us as Jesus promised (John 17:22), because we are one with Him.

Now, whether you are feeling selfish or selfless today, these two things should offer you *tremendous* hope! If your eyes are only on yourself, turn them towards what Jesus has promised for you in the coming kingdom, realizing you are being given more than you could ever dream if you will just persevere to the end! And if you're in a place spiritually where you can lay yourself aside and really seek God with all your heart, you will rejoice beyond measure in the honor that *God* is going to receive one day when all that He has purposed in and through His Son and His people will be accomplished, when His will for the world is at last done on earth as it is in heaven, fully answering the Lord's prayer! At last, the glory of the Lord will fill the earth as the waters cover the sea (Habakkuk 2:14), and when it does, the unfathomable goodness of God will overwhelm and satisfy the deepest yearning of every soul. This hope is infinitely *worthy* of our attention today and must become the goal of our existence. It needs to become what we wake up to and what we live for moment by moment. We need to eat, sleep, and breathe this hope. If we can learn to do that, we will have the abundant life Jesus promised, the life that countless brothers and sisters throughout the ages have discovered in some of the most difficult circumstances imaginable. They are able to live otherworldly lives because they live with their eyes fixed on another world.

Hope Through Trials

The Romans 5 passage about hope goes on to say that we not only rejoice because of where we fix our eyes, but we rejoice as we endure tribulations. It is possible to turn our hearts so fully to this hope at the end of the age that we can reinterpret reality now to reflect what God says about it rather than what we naturally feel about it in the flesh. For example, I think we all recognize that perseverance is a good thing. When a marathon runner finishes a race, all of us normal people who hate running are amazed, saying, "wow, what *endurance*, that's a dedicated athlete." We value the ability *to keep going* that they've gained through the constant challenges of the training regime to which they've committed themselves. Because they challenged their bodies again and again in ever-increasing measure, they developed physical and mental perseverance through the pain and struggles involved in running. Now, if that runner unexpectedly pulled a hamstring or twisted their ankle during the marathon and *still* finished the race, we would be all the more amazed, and we would celebrate that they had overcome that much more on their way to the goal. So it is with life. When "tribulations" or challenges come in life through difficult or unexpected circumstances, it produces perseverance. Getting through trials make us more able to get through the next one, and overcoming lesser challenges prepares us for the greater ones that lie ahead. If we did not face earlier challenges and get through them, we would not survive when the bigger challenges of life come to us. We can set our minds on this truth and begin to come to an acceptance of trials as "helpful." Difficult things make us stronger. Even the world realizes this, though they do their best to avoid those difficult things despite the realization. But for the Christian, we can take a higher road.

We can embrace difficulty with a view to what comes *through* perseverance. Romans 5 told us that trials produce perseverance, and perseverance produces *character*. This English word may have various meanings depending on the context in which it is used, but the word translated *here* as "character" is the proven character of something that has been tested. The idea here is the true nature of a metal which is proven through the testing of fire. The verse moves on to say that this proven, tested character produces "hope." And what is that? What is biblical hope? It's very similar to what we often think of as hope and use the word for in everyday conversations, but with a *very* important distinction. In general, "hope" involves looking forward to something good on the horizon. Unfortunately, however, we often use the term "hope" even if we highly doubt something will come our way, such as "I hope it will be a good day. Yesterday wasn't." This hope described in Romans 5, however, is *confident expectation*. We are talking about *knowing* that good is coming so deeply and certainly that you can move ahead in confidence to pursue God's promises and obey His commands no matter how difficult things get. Paul is saying if we will face hard times with Jesus and a redeemed mindset, those hard times will strengthen us to endure more, produce in us a proven character that cannot be shaken, and yield a confident expectation of good things to come because *we will have seen God come through* time and again. We'll know without a doubt that He can do it again, and the Holy Spirit within us will empower that faith when it wanes through any and every circumstance.

It is this kind of hope—born from trials—that make our brethren in Nigeria able to wake up in the morning and go to work knowing the threats that face their families from Muslim terrorists. It is this kind of hope that made Richard Wurmbrand (founder of Voice of the Martyrs) able to endure daily torture—including at one point a hot poker thrust through his abdomen—rather than revealing information about other Christians to buy his freedom. This hope is what empowers the Christians mentioned in the book of Revelation to cling to Jesus until their death by beheading at the hands of antichrist forces. It also is the only hope we can grasp which can carry us through all we will face in our own lives. It can enable us to keep working when we are dead tired and unappreciated. It can help us to keep loving when everyone mistreats us. It can strengthen us to share the Good News of Jesus with others who appear to want nothing to do with it and who criticize us for holding to it. This hope can conquer the forces of darkness and transform lives! And we need more of it. So we need to learn to endure trials with a whole new perspective, Christ's perspective. As we learn to *put on* Christ's perspective, we will learn to live with hope.

Prayer Response

"Father, my eyes are set on horizons far too low. I hear your Word on suffering a fighting and running with an eye for the prize of glory at the end of the age, and my heart falters. In moments, I turn towards something like a good meal or a better paycheck. So I ask you, Lord, increase my vision. Lift my eyes. Grow my heart until it is large enough to hold true hope. Tear my eyes away from things that fade, and fix them on the light of the Gospel in the face of Jesus Christ. Give me truly Christian hope to express to the world, the hope that led men and women throughout history to willingly sacrifice their hopes, dreams, and lives for the sake of the Son. Teach me to live for another world, that I might shine like a star in this one."

Chapter 13

Time to Get Dressed

"...we groan, earnestly desiring to be clothed with our habitation which is from heaven, if indeed, having been clothed, we shall not be found naked. For we who are in this tent groan, being burdened, not because we want to be unclothed, but further clothed, that mortality may be swallowed up by life." — 2 Corinthians 5:2-4

WHAT DOES HOPE DO FOR PEOPLE? It keeps them moving. That's why depressed (hopeless) people get to the point where they don't want to get out of bed. There is no confident expectation that good is coming, so it's easy to say, "why do anything anymore?" But hope gives them something to expect and moves them to action. The powerful, biblical hope we have been talking about *really* motivates. It has power! When God's children have it, they are moved to obedience. And that's where clothing comes in. Let's return to the main idea of this whole book: purification. We want to be purified so that when Jesus comes back, He sees what He deserves to see, a pure Bride waiting for Him. And as with any bride, one major mark of the Bride Jesus is longing to see is her devotion expressed through a beautiful, white dress that she took painstaking care to prepare, whether by sewing it herself or working long hours to purchase it. The biblical hope that dwells within us is an earnest, joyful expectation for our Groom's soon return, and it moves us to clothe ourselves properly for that day.

As we have discovered earlier in this book, the clothing for the Bride in Revelation 19 is the righteous deeds of the saints. It is *granted* to the saints to clothe themselves in this way, which references the reality that their righteous deeds are only counted because God graciously allows them to count for something through the finished work of Christ that covers them and makes them truly righteous. Without that, our deeds would be filthy rags. But with Jesus's own righteousness covering us, we can live as members of Jesus's righteous Body on earth doing righteous deeds that truly do bring Him glory and that will adorn us with beautiful clothing at the wedding feast. So what does that look like?

Let's look at where the Word speaks directly on clothing and unclothing ourselves spiritually. Paul addresses the matter in Ephesians 4 as he urges the church not to walk in darkness like they used to, but rather to cling to what they learned of Jesus, *"that you put off, concerning your former conduct, the old man which grows corrupt according to the deceitful lusts, and be renewed in the spirit of your mind, and that you put on the new man which was created according to God, in true righteousness and holiness"* (Ephesians 4:22-24). When the Word says "put off" here, it speaks of getting rid of something, as you would a filthy garment or piece of trash. The connotation, however, is that it is not to come back. It does not *belong* anymore. We are to completely throw away the old, selfish, sinful person we used to be in order to claim our new identity. As long as we cling to some measure of the old, we are missing out on some measure of the new. Two people can't inhabit the same space at the same time, and old me and new me cannot occupy the same space inside of me. They will each take territory as does an advancing army, and it is our job to make sure the old man is constantly losing ground on the way to utter defeat on the day Jesus returns to fully vanquish him. Having called us *away* from something, God then calls us *to* something, a reality which is *always* true in the Christian life. If you think you got saved *from* sin, you had better believe you were saved *for* God and His kingdom purposes.

God calls to put away the old man and to "put on" the new

man. This speaks directly of clothing, being the same term used to sink into a garment. Imagine a big one-piece robe or tunic getting draped about you until it envelops you. God is asking us to firmly grasp this new identity *in Christ* as though it were a garment and cover ourselves with it entirely until our nakedness is no longer visible and the world can see the beauty of the King upon us. Only then can we truly represent Him as members of *His* Body on the earth. Otherwise, the only thing the world can see is us. They can't see Jesus if we don't clothe ourselves in Him. Notice, too, that the Word here says the new man was created by God in true righteousness and holiness. This is a new identity for you and for me that God formed *in and through* Jesus who alone is righteous, but it is not Jesus *only*. It is also a *new you*. As is often said, this new person is who Jesus would be if He were you. You get to put on a unique understanding of yourself that reflects the image of Christ in a very particular way suited to the way He made you, and it doesn't necessarily matter what you were like before meeting Him. Some of your God-designed personality may remain, but it will be sanctified by the resurrected life of Christ in you and take on whole new shades of beauty and meaning. As the Word says, *"we are His workmanship, created in Christ Jesus for good works, which God prepared beforehand that we should walk in them"* (Eph. 2:10).

A Victorious Struggle

This putting off of the old and putting on of the new is both final and continual. Paul says to the Colossian church, *"you died, and your life is hidden with Christ in God"* (Colossians 3:3), but he also has to repeatedly rebuke, correct, and encourage this church and others who appear to be forgetting that reality. In this very same letter, he doesn't just treat it as final that their old identity has died and tell them to accept it and move on. No, he goes on to urge them to put off the old man in specific ways and to put on the new in specific ways, knowing that this will be a lifelong process. Thankfully, we can be *"confident of this very thing, that He who has begun a good work in you will complete it until the day of Jesus Christ,"* (Philippians 1:6), because *"it is God who works in you both to will and to do for His good pleasure"* (Philippians 2:13). It will be alright in the end, because Jesus will make it so, but until then, we have a daily work to do. Practically, this looks like putting off old qualities and putting on new ones through abiding in Christ. So when Paul in Colossians 3 makes it clear that we have died and been raised with Jesus, he then says, *"therefore put to death your members which are on the earth: fornication, uncleanness, passion, evil desire, and covetousness, which is idolatry"* (Colossians 3:5). We get to see some of the character of the old man, the self-centered, worldly character which reflects the kingdom of Satan who lives entirely for himself and whose pride in himself led him to the disobedience that got him kicked out of God's throne room in the first place. This selfish, rebellious character warrants God's just judgement, as Paul warns *"because of these things the wrath of God is coming upon the sons of disobedience, in which you yourselves once walked when you lived in them"* (Colossians 3:6-7). We may have once walked in those shoes and worn those clothes, but we *can't* anymore: *"...now you yourselves are to put off all these: anger, wrath, malice, blasphemy, filthy language out of your mouth. Do not lie to one another, since you have put off the old man with his deeds"* (Colossians 3:8). Jesus faced judgment for our sins, so we can't live as those who deserve judgment anymore. We must now live as those who have been rescued. When you get out of prison, you don't want to keep living like an inmate.

Really look at your life. How much of these clothes to you wear? How often do you put them on? Is anger a well-worn coat that you carry with you as you go about your day, keeping it handy in case you need to protect yourself from the winds of circumstance? Do you keep filthy language in a drawer nearby like a glove ready to handle something dirty or distasteful? Do you slip in and out of lies every morning like you do your underclothes? The answer should be a resounding "No! I can't do that anymore, because Jesus bought me with His very life!" If you struggle with these things, you are no different than any other person, but in Christ, the struggle is a *victorious* one. You are deliberately and steadily putting off these old clothes and putting on new ones, and just like physical clothes, no matter how many times your clothes get dirty, *you do it again.* The difference is, our spiritual clothing only becomes more and more permanent until the day

Jesus returns. And thank God for that! So what do we put on? Paul goes on: *"put on the new man who is renewed in knowledge according to the image of Him who created him"* (Colossians 3:10). Unlike the old man whose only concern is with his own image, this new man is made in the image of God and is consumed with the glorious purpose of displaying the character of God who made him. And it looks like this:

> *"...as the elect of God, holy and beloved, put on tender mercies, kindness, humility, meekness, longsuffering; bearing with one another, and forgiving one another, if anyone has a complaint against another; even as Christ forgave you, so you also must do. But above all these things put on love, which is the bond of perfection. And let the peace of God rule in your hearts, to which also you were called in one body; and be thankful. Let the word of Christ dwell in you richly in all wisdom, teaching and admonishing one another in psalms and hymns and spiritual songs, singing with grace in your hearts to the Lord. And whatever you do in word or deed, do all in the name of the Lord Jesus, giving thanks to God the Father through Him"* (Colossians 3:12-17).

We are to clothe ourselves with tender mercies. Doesn't that just sound so unlike most of what we get in the world (and most of what we give, for that matter)? This speaks of having compassion for others, feeling for them as they struggle and not wanting to give them what they deserve but seeking rather to treat them with kindness due to how fragile we know they really are (because of how fragile we know that *we* really are). This is a quality that belongs entirely to Jesus, who stopped to listen to beggars and touched lepers no one would come near, who used His abundance to bless all who were in need, no matter the need. This Jesus has been handed all judgment by the Father and will be the one who punishes all wickedness on the last day at the end of the age, but He gently dealt with every person he met, those who had faith and those who did not, because He understood our frame, remembering that we are dust as the Psalmist says. So when we put on a quality like tender mercy, we put on a wedding garment that will match the splendor of our groom on the wedding day because it comes from Him. So it is with all of the other qualities listed here: humility, longsuffering, forgiveness, thankfulness, and love. These are qualities exemplified in the person of Jesus as He lived and walked on earth, manifesting His glory to us so that we might see and know Him as He is. We can put on humility willingly and with joy, because we know that Jesus lowered Himself to the place of servanthood by washing feet when He was honestly King of all and deserved the whole world's devotion. We can suffer long, because Jesus suffered long for us, for 33 years in the weakness of the flesh along with thousands of years of patience in heaven beforehand, not to mention enduring the limitless agony of the cross as God's wrath for untold centuries of sin from billions of people was poured out upon Him. We can forgive, because we have been forgiven. We can be thankful, because Jesus gave thanks for even a morsel of bread just before He died when all He wanted in the flesh was to be set free from the suffering of that hour (Matthew 26:39). And we can love unconditionally, because He first loved us. He seeks our highest good and spares no expense in doing it. So must we put on love. But it's all only possible by the Holy Spirit.

If these qualities are clothes on our wedding day, then the Holy Spirit is our tailor. We'll need Him to make our clothes and help us put them on. You can try with all you've got to be good and do good, but in the morning, when you wake up, you're still going to act like a fool a large chunk of the time, and you're going to hurt people. "Picking yourself up by your bootstraps" is a funny, impossible-sounding phrase for a reason: it *is* impossible. Because of gravity, the laws of physics, and human limitations, you really can't grab your own bootstraps and lift yourself off of the ground. God made this clear physically so we would get the point spiritually, but for some reason, we all agree with the physical reality wholeheartedly while passionately ignoring the spiritual truth to the point that we live our whole lives trying to lift ourselves to heaven. Self-reliance and selfishness is ingrained in your flesh, and it won't be completely gone until you put off the flesh entirely to get a new, sinless, resurrection Body like Jesus received when He left the tomb. But until then, we have received the Holy Spirit as a guarantee that we will inherit that new Body (Ephesians 1:13-14). And *He* can produce what we never could. The Word says, *"Walk in the Spirit, and you shall not fulfill the desires of the flesh...the fruit of the Spirit is love, joy, peace, longsuffering, kindness, goodness, faithfulness, gentleness, self-control"* (Galatians 5:16-23). We are promised that when we walk by the Spirit, we will be able to put off the old man and his dastardly deeds, and we will be able to produce the fruits of the Spirit, which notably are the very same sorts of things we are told to "put on" or clothe ourselves with in Colossians 3. The Spirit makes it all possible. He buys the material, sews the clothes, and moves our hands in obedience to put them on. We need only surrender ourselves to Him and give Him our mind and heart. In the end, it's all about the heart.

Notably, these new clothes express the kingdom of God by taking on the character of God. Character begets action, and it all begins in the heart. Jesus said, *"out of the abundance of the heart, the mouth speaks,"* (Luke 6:45), because He wanted people to understand that what is in a person is inevitably what will come out of them and what the world will see. No one can speak evil or good unless it first appears in their hearts and makes its way to their lips. This is why the man who had all the wisdom of the world once wrote, *"Keep your heart with all vigilance, for from it flow the springs of life"* (Proverbs 4:23, ESV). He had been around the block a few times and realized every time he got into trouble it was because of his heart. He had bad thoughts and bad desires that manifested as bad actions and ruined his life. He knew this because God gave him wisdom, but it was another thing entirely to be set free from the cycle. Only Jesus could do that, and Solomon in his day did not know this Messiah's saving power. Jesus is able to transform the heart by the creative power that wrought the world and overcame the grave. It is His power that we must rely upon if we are to become the sort of people who do righteous deeds to clothe ourselves for the marriage supper. If we let God reign in our hearts, He will reign in our hands and cause us to do what is truly good. We will be able to do right things because visions of God will fill our minds and passion for God's character to be displayed will fill our hearts. And at long last, as we allow God to master the very seat of our being, we will see the world change around us while we work hand-in-hand with the Creator. We will see the fruits of life brought into the world through Jesus living within us, and it is then that we will know we are preparing for ourselves a proper entry to the wedding supper of the Lamb.

Obedience is Required

Ultimately, it all comes down to obedience. We show God we love Him by obeying His Word, as Jesus said point-blank to His disciples, *"If you love me, keep my commandments"* (John 14:15). But the obedience must come from a heart that truly seeks after and trusts God alone. This is why all those who thought they'd done great things for God but did not *know* God will have the gates of heaven shut in their faces on the last day (Matthew 7:23). Jesus put it plainly: *"...this is eternal life, that they may know You, the only true God, and Jesus Christ whom You have sent"* (John 17:3). Life is found in God Himself and was manifested on earth in Jesus for all of us who needed to *see* it. When we really *meet* God and began a process of getting to know Him intimately, He takes us through a process of putting off our flesh and putting on a new identity that is one with Jesus. As that happens, we begin to act like Jesus, living out our new identity as members of His Body and manifesting His presence here on earth through real, tangible displays of His character. We do *good* things that change lives, and as the world sees these things, they give glory to God and have a chance at being transformed by Him also, as Jesus said, *"let your light so shine before men, that they may see your good works and glorify your Father in heaven"* (Matthew 5:16). The Kingdom of God comes through the heartfelt actions of the Spirit of God working through human hands. Are you a part of this? Jesus helps us understand practically what this looks like here, as He shares what it will look like when all of us meet Him at the end of our time:

> *"When the Son of Man comes in His glory, and all the holy angels with Him, then He will sit on the throne of His glory. All the nations will be gathered before Him, and He will separate*

them one from another, as a shepherd divides his sheep from the goats. And He will set the sheep on His right hand, but the goats on the left. Then the King will say to those on His right hand, 'Come, you blessed of My Father, inherit the kingdom prepared for you from the foundation of the world: for I was hungry and you gave Me food; I was thirsty and you gave Me drink; I was a stranger and you took Me in; I was naked and you clothed Me; I was sick and you visited Me; I was in prison and you came to Me.' Then the righteous will answer Him, saying, 'Lord, when did we see You hungry and feed You, or thirsty and give You drink? When did we see You a stranger and take You in, or naked and clothe You? Or when did we see You sick, or in prison, and come to You?' And the King will answer and say to them, 'Assuredly, I say to you, inasmuch as you did it to one of the least of these My brethren, you did it to Me.' Then He will also say to those on the left hand, 'Depart from Me, you cursed, into the everlasting fire prepared for the devil and his angels: for I was hungry and you gave Me no food; I was thirsty and you gave Me no drink; I was a stranger and you did not take Me in, naked and you did not clothe Me, sick and in prison and you did not visit Me.' Then they also will answer Him, saying, 'Lord, when did we see You hungry or thirsty or a stranger or naked or sick or in prison, and did not minister to You?' Then He will answer them, saying, 'Assuredly, I say to you, inasmuch as you did not do it to one of the least of these, you did not do it to Me.' And these *will go away into everlasting punishment, but the righteous into eternal life'"* (Matthew 25:31-46).

Jesus draws a clear line in the sand. You will inherit the kingdom prepared for you from before the foundation of the world, or you will join the devil and his angels in everlasting fire which was prepared for them. One of these two things will happen at the end of your time on earth once judgment day arrives. As we often hear, Jesus is the way to the first. He has said, *"God did not send His Son into the world to condemn the world, but that the world through Him might be saved. Whoever believes in Him is not condemned; but whoever does not believe is condemned already, because he has not believed in the name of the only begotten Son of God"* (John 3:17-18). This is truth, and you can—and should—stake your life on it. But look at what Jesus says about the judgment seat in the above passage. Does it sound like He is evaluating whether you prayed a prayer to receive Him or believed something someone told you about Him? There is not a *hint* of a mention of it. Instead, He makes it clear that He is evaluating you based on whether you did things that *proved* you knew Him. Knowing Jesus changes things. It changes people. If you know Him, you will begin to do things in the real world that demonstrate He is living and breathing inside of *you*. God will come to earth in some measure within you. On the other hand, if you *don't* know Him, this won't happen, and that, too, is evident. It will be obvious by the things you *don't* do that you have not been with Jesus. Do you see why the Bible works so hard to let us know we need to "work out our own salvation with fear and trembling?" The world should see God's light in me through righteous deeds done in selflessness for other people.

When I see a hungry person, I should feed them. Since we don't live constantly surrounded by third-world needs here in the West, we can ignore these sorts of passages far too easily. But even in the spiritual realm, this is true. Clearly, Jesus didn't see too much separation between the spiritual and the physical when it came to meeting needs. A paralyzed guy wanted to walk, so Jesus forgave him of his sins. Onlookers may have thought that was foolish, but the man *needed* that forgiveness to live out his days with hope. Jesus also healed the man's body, because that can matter too even though it won't last. He showed compassion through action. There are prisoners in the world, and most of us never see them unless we are related to them or work in law enforcement. And yet, Jesus says that He can know we mean business in our commitment to Him by whether we visit prisoners. It's pretty straightforward on one hand: visiting physical, concrete prisons are a good way to show Jesus you love Him. It's also deeper. Surrounding you are people imprisoned by grief, fear, depression, addiction, and the like, and Jesus is fully capable of setting them free by His resurrection power and the Good News of His finished work on the cross. We can visit these people in their difficulty and share this hope with them. We can set them free! And the thirsty? If we live in the desert, we should give them water. Everyone else needs the living water, Jesus Christ, and they are *dying* of thirst all around us!

The fact is, we ignore Scriptures that we think we can't obey on the spot, and that is because we are impatient, selfish fools who want to live to build our own kingdoms. But when a person joins themselves to the Son of God in covenant partnership, this all has to change, day by day, bit by bit. The Holy Spirit comes to take up residence in us, and He does not enter an environment that He does not change. His very presence is reality-forming, as it was at the beginning of the world when He hovered over the waters of the unformed globe and from Him came all the life we now see. He will lead us to do right things as we follow Him, and those right things will form the clothes we wear when we enter His presence at the moment we have all been waiting for, when we are at last fully accepted and loved in an environment without fear or worry. You *want* to be well-presented on that day. It will be precious beyond words. If you don't grasp these words, if you choose not to cultivate the soil of your soul so that it can receive this clear message from God's Word, you may end up like the man described in 1 Corinthians 3:9-15, who built on the foundation of Jesus Christ with *other things* that will not stand on judgement day. The Word says that he himself will be saved, but as though through fire, and all his works will be burned up.

Whether this means you will show up naked to the wedding feast, I do not know. In the parable about the wedding feast in the Gospels, Jesus seems to say that those who try coming in without a wedding garment don't get in. You will have to go to God and determine this for yourself. I will simply say that you should be amazed there is a chance of still being saved if you do not live a life full of righteous deeds now. Our Savior is *that* amazing, and God is *that* compassionate, as God's Word says, *"Let the wicked forsake his way, and the unrighteous man his thoughts; let him return to the Lord, and He will have mercy on him; and to our God, for He will abundantly pardon. 'For My thoughts are not your thoughts, nor are your ways My ways,' says the Lord. 'For as the heavens are higher than the earth, so are My ways higher than your ways, and My thoughts than your thoughts"* (Isaiah 55:7-9). God is so much more compassionate than we are, He has to use a distance of thousands of miles to communicate the difference. He will be good to you. The question is, will you be good to Him? Let us heed the Words of Jesus, and be purified:

> *"Therefore whoever hears these sayings of Mine, and does them, I will liken him to a wise man who built his house on the rock: and the rain descended, the floods came, and the winds blew and beat on that house; and it did not fall, for it was founded on the rock. But everyone who hears these sayings of Mine, and does not do them, will be like a foolish man who built his house on the sand:*

and the rain descended, the floods came, and the winds blew and beat on that house; and it fell. And great was its fall" (Matthew 7:24-27).

Prayer Response

"God, I'm so thankful I was baptized into Christ. I am confident that His death was final for the old me, and his resurrection was final for the new me. Both cannot dwell together anymore. I choose to put off the old and put on the new. Strengthen me by your might to do this again and again, daily taking up the cross of Christ to crucify that man who would stop up the well of living water within me. Take this old heart of stone that cares nothing for my brother, and clothe me in compassion. Throw away selfish ambition, and give me godly ambition, a thirst for the greatness of your name! Remove this rough, violent nature and replace it with the strength of gentle patience. Begin to clothe me in righteous deeds for the last day so I can be beautiful for your arrival. Give me opportunities to shine your light before men, and empower me to proclaim and live out the truth. Lead me to do justice, love mercy, and walk humbly with you, God. Let that evidence of a life changed by Christ be what tells the world He lives. Receive me on the last day in splendor, a purified bride for a worthy Bridegroom. Amen!"

Epilogue

The huge live-oak table sat upon a shimmering sea of crystal stretching on endlessly into the sunset, its transparent surface reflecting the constant flashes of light that danced all about. The aroma of roasting meat mingled with the sweet fragrance of ten thousand roses as creatures clothed in light brought tray after tray of the finest food to the table: boneless porterhouse steak, shell-less buttered lobster, handmade Italian pasta, curry that never hurt the tongue, tureens of every kind of soup, and cakes and pies from every nation under heaven. It was a truly indescribable feast! As the servants worked, a million joyful shouts thundered across the diamond expanse but somehow didn't shake the golden goblets of fine wine set carefully at every place. It was a joyous occasion, and every soul was bursting with excitement, none more so than the one seated on the throne at the head of the table.

The throne appeared to be crafted entirely of the purest sapphire, wreathed in flame and born upon wheels of fire. Enshrouded in a living rainbow, the Lord of the earth sat, Himself blazing with purest light, the Light of the World. A robe as white as moonlit snow hung on His shoulders, spilling over the fiery sides of the throne unsinged and filling the entire room. His figure itself was colossal beyond belief, radiating heat like gleaming, molten metal, like burnished bronze encasing flame. Bright, luminous orbs that appeared to be stars rested easily in His grip, and the hair falling down the back of His robe was white as finest wool. His face shone like the sun in full strength, and His eyes were a living flame, burning into the soul, buckling the knees in worshipful obedience, and both urging the onlooker to flee from His presence and inviting them to bask in it all at once. In those eyes one could see the indomitable will that brought forth existence, and it commanded praise.

It would have been a worthy occasion if all of it was only for the King on the throne, but this was no ordinary day in heaven's courts—no, it was the marriage supper of the Lamb. Finally, the Lamb who was slain would have the reward for His sufferings: He would have His Bride. She would be His, and He would be hers, and nothing would separate them for all eternity. With this unspeakable joy on His mind, the Groom heard the sound of the gates opening. She had come at last! The sky shone with a myriad stars like a diamond-studded sheet of black satin, a glorious backdrop for the stark white form that emerged from between the glittering pearl gates. Angelic musicians started up in earnest, serenading the betrothed with a heavenly melody that made the soul soar. And the Groom's soul was soaring! The moment the gates opened, He had leapt from His place in a mighty flash of light, His presence blazing brighter still as joy overtook Him. He streaked like a shooting star towards His lady. At last, they could be together!

She was stunning, the picture of modest grace. Clothed in

intricately-woven white lace from head to toe, her gown glimmered with the light of the surrounding stars, and she only grew brighter as the Groom drew nearer. As she met with the cacophonous applause of the gathered hosts of heaven, she turned away slightly, hiding her face shyly behind her veil, but it did not conceal her beaming smile at the sight of her beloved across the room. In a moment, however, He had spanned the distance between them, and He swept her up in His arms, twirling her about and sending flecks of light flying in every direction as her shimmering train swirled behind them. He held her easily aloft for the longest time before carefully setting her back on her feet. The bride looked into the Groom's eyes, and His burning gaze overwhelmed her with love as He said, "I love you, my dear. I've always loved you. You are mine now, and I am yours. We must celebrate!" With that, He sprung into a lively jig, feet whirling as He sang aloud of His devotion. You wouldn't have expected it of any other King, but for Him, the Author of joy, it was only too fitting.

His excitement expressed, the Groom returned to His Bride's side and took her gently by the hand. "Now," He whispered, "I want to show you something." Before the Bride could breathe again, they were away, spirited off into the sunset. But what came next nearly took her breath away. She was standing atop a mountain peak arm-in-arm with her Beloved, and He touched her cheek to direct her gaze towards a particular spot in the sky. As she turned, she was nearly blinded by the dazzling glare of light refracting through what appeared to be...*a diamond city*. She couldn't believe her eyes. Most ladies would have been delighted for a diamond ring, but her Groom had gone above and beyond to display His affection. And the sight was only getting better. When her eyes had adjusted, she saw that not only was she looking at diamond walls stretching for miles, she could also see every other gemstone studding the foundations of the walls, creating a stunning display of living color as light bounced endlessly from one stone to another. And within the city, buildings made of what looked like pure gold soared off into soft pink clouds above, each of them transparent as glass.

"It's for you, my love," the Groom said with tears in His eyes. "I've been waiting to give it to you for so very long, and it won't be finished until you fill it with the brightness of your beauty." He then threw His arm out to the side in a grand sweeping gesture, continuing, "And look, I have made all things new. This is a new heaven and earth, and it's all for you. Here, there will be no need of a sun, because I will always be here to give it light. Here, you won't ever cry again. There won't be a reason! We'll be able to enjoy all that we have together forever." She was speechless. What love was this? She couldn't believe it, even as she looked into His eyes and saw the majesty and unshakeable confidence that assured her it was so. She and He, together, so it would always be...

And they lived happily ever after.

A Word from the Author

If you've finished this book, then you should have some idea of what God is saying to His people in this critical hour of the world. This book was a work of the Holy Spirit, inspired not precisely as the Scriptures were inspired (I'd never claim its inerrancy) but inspired nonetheless. It came to me as I wrote it, and anytime I would ask God what else to write, He would oblige. Every time I read it for any purpose at all, I get convicted by the sure testimony of the Word of God.

All of this is to say if you were convicted by your reading of *Purified*, then you stand convicted by no man but by the Lord of the Earth, your Maker, and you will be held accountable for what you've read on Judgment Day. You have a chance to come face to face with Jesus and be changed. If you read the book too fast to do that, treating it more like a novel than a devotional book, then please, go back through the book slowly and deliberately with the goal of connecting with God. To behold Him is to be transformed, but we must *behold* Him.

If, on the other hand, you took the time to encounter the Living God, then I have but one Word left for you. *"The grace of God has appeared, bringing salvation for all people, training us to renounce ungodliness and worldly passions, and to live self-controlled, upright, and godly lives in the present age, waiting for our blessed hope, the appearing of the glory of our great God and Savior Jesus Christ, who gave himself for us to redeem us from all lawlessness and to purify for* *himself a people for his own possession who are zealous for good works"* (Titus 2:11-14). Take firm hold of this grace and begin to live for another world. Wait for your blessed hope with all you are, and be zealous for good works. Jesus deserves it! And He gives more grace. Remember, He is the true prize* (Hebrews 13:5).

In Christ,

Jonathan Macnab

P.S. If you don't have this prize* by now, you'd better change course quickly. His mercy is new every morning, but one day, morning won't come.

Help Spread the Word

If you believe in the message of this book or the Scriptures contained within, you can help be a part of increasing the Word of God in the world and increasing the faith that comes through hearing the Word. Please review the book at Amazon.com or wherever you can so that the book becomes higher recommended and easier to find for potential readers.

Please also consider some of the following uses of the book:

* Share the FREE e-book link (https://books2read.com/u/baDNBa) on your social media with a personal message about its content.
* Present it to someone you meet out and about or to someone visiting your home.
* Leave it in barber shops, waiting rooms, offices, etc.
* Put a print copy in your church library or offer it as a free discipleship resource.
* Forward it to a prison, to sailors, soldiers, firemen, and others with standby time and a need for good material.
* Make a list of friends or acquaintances who should read the book, then send the book to the first named and ask them to pass it on to the second, and so on.
* Call the attention of your local bookseller to it and urge them to carry a line of books from the same publisher.
* Read it aloud to your children or other young people.

About the Author

Thank you for taking the time to read this book. It was a labor of love with my Heavenly Father, and I trust He will use it to bless you as surely as He used it to bless me. My hope is that He is glorified through it as more and more people turn towards Him in loving obedience. I can't tell you just how much of this book is still being worked out in my own life. It's amazing to think that I was even able to write it with all the selfishness rising up in me and getting in the way of what the Spirit wanted to do. But I trust God's Word does not return void, and it is accomplishing what He sent it out to do.

I want you to know that anything praiseworthy you find in this book belongs to the King, and you should give Him praise rather than giving me accolades. At best, I was an obedient servant. At worst, I mangled what He wanted to present to the world, and He let me help still like a gentle father lets his child help even if it ruins his work. Even so, this is only the beginning of what we will do together, He and I. He has many more books, both nonfiction and fiction for both adults and children, that He wants to write with me. And for that, I am thankful. If you want to walk with me on this journey to discover what He has for us, I welcome you.

In me, you will find a simple man who loves God, his family, and being creative with words. I am passionate to see the Church become the unstoppable force Jesus intended it to be in our time, and I will write and preach whatever it takes to help us reach that goal. I recognize that each of us is both a magnificent masterpiece and a terrible wretch, and I long to see and love people the way Jesus loves me. He sees past it all, and He sticks around. What a Savior!

Connect With Me

I hope you enjoyed the book! Please support the work by leaving a review at amazon.com or goodreads.com. If you have any thoughts or questions, feel free to contact me on my Facebook page "Story Reborn". You can also email me at jonathan@storyreborn.com.

Visit my blog at www.storyreborn.com and consider joining the email list to gain access to book samples and even advanced book copies. You'll be able to see regular updates on upcoming books as well as inspiring articles on literature and truth.

www.ingramcontent.com/pod-product-compliance
Lightning Source LLC
Chambersburg PA
CBHW020527080526
44583CB00013B/767